CONCORDE: THE CASE AGAINST SUPERSONIC TRANSPORT

FRIENDS OF THE EARTH was founded in 1969 in America by David R. Brower and in 1970 in the United Kingdom. It is a non-profit-making organization created to undertake aggressive political and legislative activity aimed at restoring an environment misused by man. FOE invites your participation.

> We seek a renewed stirring of love for the earth; we urge that what man is capable of doing to the earth is not always what he ought to do; and we plead that all people here, now, determine that a wide, spacious untrammelled freedom shall remain as living testimony that this generation, our own, had love for the next.
>
> David R. Brower

Address:

Friends of the Earth Ltd
8 King Street,
London, WC2
Telephone: (01)836 0718

CONCORDE:
THE CASE AGAINST SUPERSONIC TRANSPORT

RICHARD WIGGS

Foreword by Michael Foot, MP

A BALLANTINE
FRIENDS OF THE EARTH BOOK PUBLISHED IN
ASSOCIATION WITH PAN BOOKS LTD
33 TOTHILL ST., LONDON, S.W.1

First published in Great Britain 1971

ISBN 0 345 02138 X

Printed in Great Britain by
Cox & Wyman Ltd, London, Reading and Fakenham

CONTENTS

FOREWORD BY MICHAEL FOOT, MP

One fine day in the month of July 1967, I received a letter from a Richard Wiggs, who was entirely unknown to me, to ask whether I would join in sponsoring his Anti-Concorde Project. I knew almost as little about Anti-Concorde as about Richard Wiggs. But his letter enlisted my instincts. What little I did know about Concorde had persuaded me it was a prize technological monstrosity, the latest example of how scientific brilliance could be fatuously mis-applied. So, while making it clear that other activities would prevent me from being an active campaigner, I joined the campaign.

Since then I have watched with great and growing admiration one of the most remarkable contests since David fought Goliath. For, according to the modern tests which are sometimes accepted without debate, Concorde had everything on its side. Fabulous and literally incalculable sums of money were committed to the project, which meant in turn that scarcely less-fabulous sums would be available for the publicity machine to defend it against all attacks and criticisms. Governments and Oppositions on both sides of the Channel and of varying complexions were committed. Indeed, they were tied up in what appeared to be an inextricable legal tangle, as the Labour Cabinet discovered when it made its attempt to escape in October 1964. Money, national prestige, international law, scientific pride, and what Orientals are supposed to call face, all lined up on one side. Against them Richard Wiggs and the associates he had gathered together had at their disposal little more than a sling and a few pebbles. But Goliath lost his legendary fight – and the final outcome of the present battle is still in the future. Even if the maniac giant should win this time, the story of this battle should encourage those who would be on the side of civilization to muster themselves earlier, to commit themselves more unreservedly.

The prospect at the precise moment of the publication of

this book is more enticing than that. The fate of Concorde either hangs in the balance or is still being anxiously debated by technology-entranced Conservative Ministers. All the points which have figured in Richard Wiggs' successive bulletins have been or are being pored over by the most highly-placed and highly-paid civil servants, who should have been doing their poring before. But better late than never. They will still have the chance to save several hundreds of millions, however many hundreds of millions may already have gone down the drain. They are hard at it making some of the most inscrutable calculations with which economists were ever charged. The subject of this book is the facts about supersonic airliners, and especially the facts which the advocates of these machines have been at some pains to explain away, to minimize and to conceal – the unacceptability of their sonic bangs, the tremendous noise they make at airports, the possibility that their pollution of the upper atmosphere could adversely – even disastrously – affect weather and climate, and their prodigious cost, in public money, irrecoverably spent. Who knows; the wider publication of these facts may just help to tip the balance?

And, whatever the outcome, the history of the Concorde and Anti-Concorde Projects will have its significance for decades to come. More and more, mankind will have to pick and choose between the technological possibilities available to us. More and more, at much earlier stages, we shall have to learn to apply intelligent tests. What is the real purpose behind the new projects? Will they enhance the qualities of people's lives – or will they debase them? How can ordinary people be involved in making the decisions? All too often, and excusably, the response to such large questions is a feeling of hopelessness. But, win or lose, the Anti-Concorde Project should put such attitudes to shame. And, at the moment, the wonderful signs are that we are going to win.

Michael Foot

PREFACE

Advocacy for supersonic transport has, from the beginning, been characterized by grossly inadequate estimates of its cost, by extravagant and insubstantiable claims about its benefits, and by refusal to face the facts about its anti-social effects. There has been much talk of prestige, and of profits. But what are the facts?

What are the effects of the sonic bang? Will supersonic flight overland be banned? Would the noise of supersonic airliners be even more intolerable than present-day aircraft noise, to people living near airports? Is there any real need, or demand, for supersonic airliners? Is it possible for them to be operated profitably – and are the airlines likely to buy them? What are the prospects for the Concorde?

This book answers some of these questions, and gives facts upon which the answers to all of them depend.

In February 1970 Dr Shurcliff's *SST and Sonic Boom Handbook* was published in New York (Ballantine Books). Dr Shurcliff and I have been working together very closely since 1967, and now, with his permission I have freely and extensively made use of material from his book. Dr Shurcliff wishes to join me in acknowledging our immense debt to Mr B. K. O. Lundberg, for twenty years Director of the Swedish Institute for Aviation Research, from whose truly monumental efforts the international campaign to stop the SSTs has grown.

I must also mention with gratitude the supporters of the Anti-Concorde Project, on whose behalf I have been working, full-time, as organizer of the project, since 1967 – and whose financial support has made this work possible. The members of the Advisory Committee have been a constant source of help and encouragement. I would also like to thank Mr C. B. Edwards, of the Department of Economics, University of East Anglia (author of 'Concorde – a case study in cost-benefit analysis' – 1969); Air Commodore John Davis (author of 'The Concorde Affair' – Frewin, 1969) for information on the early history of the Concorde project; and Mr G. W. Searle, Chairman of the National Union of Students Committee for the Environment, for editorial assistance.

Richard Wiggs

CHAPTER ONE

The Challenge of Supersonic Transport

During the 1960s certain aircraft builders developed an obsession – not for the first time, perhaps, but this one was on an exceptional scale. It was concerned with the development, manufacture, sale and operation of vast fleets of supersonic airliners, which would carry people across the world at twice the speed of sound – faster than a rifle bullet. In recent decades the triumphs of technology had become ever more spectacular, and here was another immense challenge to human ingenuity and technological skill. The cost of developing these machines would be great – far beyond the resources of the manufacturers – so government aid was sought, and obtained. But success would bring great rewards, in foreign exchange, in prestige, in profits for the manufacturers. Long-range travel would be revolutionized: we were promised trans-Atlantic day-trips, weekends in the Antipodes. In Britain and France, the Concorde was promoted as a symbol of national prestige – we were, for once, ahead of the Americans. In the USA, the 'challenge of Concorde' meant that a bigger, faster American SST must be built.

Throughout most of the 1960s, supersonic transport was popularly presented as a great and shining symbol for the 1970s. It was, we were told, progress. It was inevitable.

Some people still believe these things. But during the late 1960s this image began to change. Doubts began to creep in. And in the latter half of 1970 the Concorde is fighting for its life. Rumours that it will imminently be cancelled, and assurances that it will not, follow one another with confusing rapidity. On 2nd December, 1970, the United States Senate voted to prohibit commercial supersonic flights over the USA, and to impose severe restrictions upon the noise of

SSTs at airports. On 3rd December, the Senate struck out the entire $290m requested by the Administration for the development of two SST prototypes. While it is likely that a much smaller amount of money will be provided, in order to avoid the complete cancellation of the SST project, the opponents of the SST have won some formidable victories. These developments, on both sides of the Atlantic, have resulted partly from the fact that the costs of the supersonic projects have risen far beyond the estimates: When the Anglo-French Concorde agreement was signed in 1962, the cost of research and development was estimated at £150m to £170m; by November 1970 this had risen to £875m, with no assurance that it will not rise further. But the change is also related to the growth, during the same period, of 'environmental' awareness. Quite suddenly, we have all become aware of 'pollution' in its many aspects. And equally suddenly the image of the SSTs[1] has changed from being the symbol of the future to being a symbol of certain bad habits which we have inherited from the past – the habits of exploitation for quick profit and short-term benefit, regardless of – indeed often ignorant of – the long-term disadvantages, and heedless of the ultimate total cost.

It becomes increasingly clear that SSTs are intolerably noisy – both at airports and on account of the 'sonic bang' which they generate throughout supersonic flight. Supersonic transport had become a focusing point – a test case – for the 'environmentalist' movement on both sides of the Atlantic.

The possibility has arisen that at some international airports SSTs will not be permitted to land. It is certain that because of the sonic bang, many countries will forbid overflying by SSTs. Restrictions on overland flight will greatly reduce the potential sales of SSTs. The manufacturers claim they can still sell large numbers of machines even on the assumption that SSTs will be allowed to fly 'only over water or sparsely populated areas'. But no one has yet produced

1. Throughout this book the term 'SST' is frequently used to denote 'supersonic transport,' including the Concorde. Wherever reference is intended to the US SST alone, this is made clear.

any reason for supposing that sonic bangs – far too severe to be tolerated by people in densely populated areas – will be acceptable to people in 'sparsely populated areas', on islands, and on ships.

Moreover the SST projects were commenced in a period when air traffic was increasing rapidly, and when it was assumed that this rapid rate of increase would continue indefinitely. This expectation has proved ill-founded – there are fewer passengers than were expected, and competing for them is a new rival: the jumbo jet.

Currently, £2½m is being spent on the Concorde per week. Already some £500m have been spent on Concorde by the British and French Governments (the manufacturers are investing no money of their own). On top of the cost of research and development (which, if the project continues, is likely to reach £1,000m), a further £300m loan from the governments to the manufacturers would be required to set up the production line. To justify putting the aircraft into quantity production a large number of orders would be required. Can these be obtained? At present there are no orders for Concordes, only reserved delivery positions (totalling 74). What are the airlines' attitudes to the prospect of 'going supersonic'?

Speaking in London in July 1969, Mr F. C. Wiser, President of Trans-World Airlines, said: 'It will be extremely difficult for any airline to make supersonic planes pay, because of their increased running costs and smaller size.'

The chairman of the board of American Airlines, General Elwood R. Quesada, told the Joint Economic Sub-Committee on Economy in Government: 'A lot of the people say the airlines wish the plane [the supersonic transport] would go away. I'm one of them' (*Washington Post* – 8th May, 1970). American Airlines operates mostly on US domestic routes. It has 6 options on Concordes. General Quesada has also invented a new term for the SSTs, including the Concorde: they would be, in commercial operation, 'non-compensatory'. This means as the *Economist* observed on 16th May, 1970, that the aircraft would be non-profit-making.

The Times ('Business News') – 13th October, 1970, reported: The coolest note yet heard from British Overseas Airways Corporation on Concorde was sounded by Mr Ross Stainton, Deputy Managing Director, in his Presidential Address to the Institute of Transport last night. 'To the airlines, it represents a tempting engineering development, but a heavy demand on limited investment funds with as yet no certainty of increased return,' he said. 'Magnificent as Concorde is as a technical achievement a rational assessment of cost and benefit has yet to be made.' BOAC, like Air France, took out options on eight Concordes some years ago at a cost now estimated at some £10m each, and have not hitherto shown any public lack of enthusiasm. To the community at large Mr Stainton said: 'Concorde has become a focus of fears that our physical environment may be threatened by the uncontrollable momentum of technology.' With Britain's increasingly scarce resources of air, space, land, and coastline, Mr Stainton suggested the setting up of a national transport planning commission.

Independent economists have attacked the SST-proponents' profitability and balance of payments claims. 'The truth is that these calculations are strictly fraudulent and should detain no one,' stated Professor J. K. Galbraith, in the USA (inserted in the *Congressional Record* by Senator Fulbright, 17th September, 1970). 'Europe is pouring £800m of its precious resources into a project that posterity may point to as the biggest technological boob of its generation.' (The *Economist*, London, 16th March, 1968.) 'Concorde will be the most expensive commercial flop the world has ever seen [concludes] a survey, prepared by London aviation consultant, Richard Worcester, of world aircraft requirements, both military and civil, between now and 1980.' (The *Observer* 'Business section', London, 4th October, 1970.) 'The new onslaught against Concorde in Britain happens to coincide with press leaks of the contents of a confidential report by M. Charles de Chambrun to the Gaullist Party on waste of government funds taking Concorde as a particularly blatant example.' (*The Times*, 2nd October, 1970.)

At the present time in the UK, the question of the future of the Concorde SST project is being widely and openly debated. Similar debate is beginning in France. The sonic bangs of the prototype Concordes have been experienced. That their intensity is far beyond the limits of acceptability, that they disturb, alarm, and terrify people and animals, and that they damage buildings, is proved. When Concorde prototype 002 made an unscheduled visit to Heathrow airport, the prodigious noise of its landing outraged people beneath its path, and damaged some of their houses. (Please see Chapter 7.)

The claimed profitability of the Concorde project is being publicly scrutinized. Arthur Reed (Air corespondent of *The Times*) wrote in the *Illustrated London News* (26th September, 1970): 'Sales of 250 Concordes at £10m a time will bring in £2,500m to be split between the two nations. But production costs will take most of that, and then there is that £730m[2] research and development money – which could escalate to £1,000m before the project is much older.' The British Minister of Trade and Industry, Mr John Davies, summed up his government's attitude to the Concorde recently: 'It will be continually under scrutiny because we cannot as a country afford to spend money on things that are not worth having. Concorde is not yet in that category.' The evidence given in this book indicates that the Concorde is, and always was, in that category.

In the USA, as the economic, profitability and balance of payments arguments in favour of the Boeing SST projects come under increasingly heavy fire from the environmentalist lobby, there has emerged a tendency to use 'the challenge of Concorde' as the spearhead of a counter-attack. Similarly in the UK and France, advocates of Concorde fear that 'if we don't do it, the Americans will'. *The Times* of 2nd October, 1970, observed. 'The fate of Concorde is inextricably woven into the fate of its American rival. The prototypes being built by Boeing are five years behind the European aircraft, but Concorde's commercial ability hinges largely on the United States completing its

2. Now £825m.

own development programme. Equally, the most telling argument in favour of the further development of the American prototypes is that supersonic flight is inevitable because of the European and Soviet aircraft.'

Almost the final argument in favour of the SST project is that they generate great technological 'spin-off' or 'fall-out' – that new materials, new techniques, etc., are developed which have valuable applications in other fields. But in a special report 3rd September, 1970) *The Engineer* (London) referred to these claims as 'dubious': 'Take Concorde for example: There is very little in this super-airliner that is of spin-off value to British industry.' And the sad fact is that while continuing to spend £1,000,000 every week on the Concorde, the UK Government is currently cutting down with utmost severity all manner of research projects, quite regardless of *their* possible spin-off.

Why were the SST projects commenced?

Was it ever seriously believed that the Concorde – which started the supersonic race – could be developed for £150m to £170m (the official estimate in 1962)? Was it not known that the SST sonic bang would be intolerable? We shall see that the sonic bang problem was well understood in the 1950s, as a result of the effects of military supersonic flying – at a time when the SST was literally no more than an improbable fantasty in the minds of a few 'advanced-aviation' specialists. The question arises – very forcibly – why were the SST projects ever started?

These questions are examined later. They are to some extent a matter of history, but, if SST is – as its opponents consider it to be – a test case in the current confrontation between environmentalists and technology-rampant, questions must be asked, and they must be answered. If the right lessons can be learned, and if they can be applied, we may get some value for our money – some measure of unexpected 'spin-off'.

CHAPTER TWO

The Beginnings of the Concorde Project

By 1955 the jet engine had revolutionized military aircraft, and was about to do the same for civil airliners. Experimental aircraft in the USA had already reached twice the speed of sound. In the USA a fighter aircraft, the F100 Super Sabre, which was capable of supersonic speeds in level flight, was being delivered to the Air Force. The British and French were building supersonic fighters; and Britain and the United States were designing supersonic bombers.

At the end of the war, civil airliners were operating at around 200 mph – a transatlantic crossing took *15 hours*. By 1955, 600 mph was in sight – the transatlantic time would be 6½ hours. The Comet had appeared; although of limited success, its showed the shape of things to come. The big American jets – the 707 and the DC8 – were soon to emerge. Following the usual pattern of events, they were closely based upon well-tried military aircraft. To some people, looking ahead and trying to make out future trends, it seemed that civil practice must surely follow military achievements again – into the supersonic speed range. But most of those who considered the question believed that supersonic civil aviation was not a viable proposition.[1] The reason for this was the cost – not so much the cost of designing and building the machine (which was thought of as high – although in fact it was vastly underestimated), as the cost of operating it. During the 1950s air fares had become cheaper. It was assumed that passengers would be willing to pay more if supersonic travel were offered, but it appeared

1. The background to the early history of the Concorde project is given in some detail in *The Concorde Affair*, by Air Commodore John Davis. (Leslie Frewin, 1969.)

that supersonic fares might be ten or twenty times as much as subsonic, which was clearly unacceptably high.

Why should supersonic operating costs be so much higher? The reason is that the physical conditions in which a supersonic aircraft operates are very different from those involving a subsonic machine. The physical conditions of supersonic flight are discussed in Chapter Three; the simple fact is that to force an aircraft through the atmosphere at speed above the speed of sound requires a vast amount of power. This has immediate results: the outside of the aircraft becomes very hot, and so special materials, and special cooling systems for the interior, become necessary.[2]

To minimize resistance to the air (known as drag) the machine must be very long and thin. To be capable of withstanding the stresses of operating at speeds faster than the speed of a rifle bullet, the aircraft must be very strong indeed. These requirements lead to weight problems, which are further compounded by the weight of the enormous quantities of fuel required. The *payload* (weight of passengers and luggage) is much smaller in SSTs than in subsonic machines, so much so that early calculations led to the conclusion that there might be almost no payload at all.

> 'In 1955 a working party at the Royal Aircraft Establishment (Farnborough) took a good look at the possibilities. It concluded that the most practicable design, for a supersonic transatlantic transport seemed to be an aircraft with thin wings, a long slender fuselage, and weighing around 340,000 pounds. It would carry the remarkable total of eighteen passengers from London to New York. Obviously the cost per passenger would be ridiculous. The only prudent conclusion was that supersonic transport was not worth pursuing.'[3]

But the members of the 'working party at the Royal Aircraft Establishment' were not content with this con-

2. Much of the energy involved is dissipated as a supersonic shock-wave (the sonic bang). (See Chapter Five.)

3. *The Concorde Affair*, p. 18.

clusion. In October 1955 Mr Philip Hufton, of Supersonic research at RAEF went to the USA for discussions; afterwards he reported that an SST operating at about Mach. 1.2 might be feasible.[4] This set off the members of the former 'working party' again. This time they looked into implications of a new shape – the *delta*. Delta-winged subsonic aircraft had previously been built and flown successfully. The RAE people knew that others, in the USA, were thinking along similar lines, so that if proposals for an SST were to be produced, they must be produced rapidly. Early in 1956 it was decided that a viable SST might be constructed – possibly a delta-wing. 'Morien Morgan, the ebullient Director of RAEF (now Sir Morien Morgan, controller of Guided Weapons and Electronics, Ministry of Technology), Hufton, and Kuchemann (Dr Dietrich Kuchemann) considered what could be done to organize a new attack on the problem.[5]

> 'The only way was to get the cooperation of the industry, the airlines, the interested ministries and Government establishments, the Air Registration Board; and for these to work together to examine the problem in depth. RAE did something about it. In the spring of 1956, they took the initiative and began to sell the idea to the Ministry of supply and the other bodies which, it was hoped, would share in the joint examination. After six months' argument and persuasion by the then Director, Mr (later Sir) George Gardiner, and his deputy, Morien Morgan, all parties agreed. In October 1956, the Supersonic Transport Aircraft Committee was formed.'[6]

On this committee (STAC) were: representatives of all the main aircraft firms and engine companies; BOAC and BEA; the Aircraft Research Establishment; the National Physical Laboratory; the National Gas Turbine Establishment; RAEF; the Ministry of Transport and Civil Aviation

4. Mach. 1 is the speed of sound in air – 700 mph at sea-level.
5. *The Concorde Affair*, p. 22.
6. *The Concorde Affair*, p. 23.

and the Ministry of Supply (the aviation responsibilities of these two ministries were later taken over by the Board of Trade and the Ministry of Technology). The chairman was Morien Morgan.

The report of the STAC is still a 'classified document', although why this is so is not clear. John Davis (*The Concorde Affair*, p. 26) writes that 'there is a probably well-founded rumour that the French were given a copy of the STAC report soon after it was written'. The significance of this emerges later. Whatever the precise contents of that report may be, the committee decided that sufficient was known to support the conclusion that SST was feasible, and it recommended two aircraft: one medium range (1,500 miles), Mach. 1.2 (800 mph) 100 passengers; the other, long-range (3,500 miles), Mach. 1.8 (1,200 mph) 150 passengers. It preferred the latter.

Since the report is still 'classified', the extent to which considerations other than aerodynamics and engineering were discussed is not known. The committee consisted entirely of technical and aviation staff. There is reason to believe that the question of the sonic bang was deliberately avoided. The STAC did consider the question of cost, and in this area its conclusions are known: the cost of research and development would be about £90m for the Mach. 1.8 aircraft (which eventually became the Concorde) and £60-£70m for the slower version; the selling price per aircraft would be £3m or £4m. On the selling price, the STAC underestimated by a factor of 3 or 4; on the R and D costs, their figure was about ten times too small. The STAC committee produced its report in March 1959. The report drew attention to the dangers of delay in getting on with designing and building a real aircraft. British industry had to get in first if it were to have a chance of getting a good share of the market.[7]

The Ministry of Supply moved (for a Ministry) with comparative rapidity; in the following September it commissioned 'feasibility studies' from the Bristol Aircraft Company (later merged into the British Aircraft Corporation) and from Hawker Siddeley Aviation. In October 1960 Mr

7. *The Concorde Affair*, p. 45.

Peter Thorneycroft, Minister of Aviation, announced that BAC had been awarded a £350,000 'limited design study' contract. The design study would be concerned with proposals for a Mach. 2.2. aircraft, to carry about 120 passengers.

> 'It is odd that Hawker Siddeley were apparently never told they had "lost". The first they heard of the result was newspaper reports that BAC had the contract. They had to ask the Ministry why they were now out of the game, and were told they had enough work on other projects.'[8]

The BAC design study was submitted to the Ministry in August 1961. It proposed a machine with six engines, with transatlantic range, to carry 130 passengers; the weight had gone up to 380,000 lb (170 tons). Apparently the Ministry was not entirely pleased. The increase in weight implied a more severe sonic bang – and the facts about the effects of the sonic bangs which would be generated by fleets of SSTs were beginning to emerge. The economics of this large machine were admittedly not good; and to have six engines would pose additional technical problems. But even before this design study was submitted to the Ministry, the Ministry had commissioned a further study of a four-engined machine from BAC. This second study was completed towards the end of 1961. The weight of this version would be 250,000 lb (111 tons); it would carry 100 passengers across the Atlantic.

In the meantime – in June 1961 – at the Paris Air Show, Sud Aviation displayed a model of the 'Super Caravelle'. Its proposed speed was Mach. 2.2; a medium range, four-engined, delta-winged aircraft, similar to the design produced by BAC a few months later.

The Americans had already been apprised of the British interest in SST by Philip Hufton's visit to the USA in October 1955; but they did not start taking a serious interest in SST development until some years later, when the Concorde was sufficiently far advanced to be used as an argument in

8. *The Concorde Affair*, p. 55, footnote.

favour of the US government supporting the development of an SST which of course had to be bigger and faster than the European SST. The Russians, not to be beaten by the Western capitalists got their SST project going and produced a machine very similar indeed to the Concorde.

Providentially, the feasibility study contracts given to Bristol and Hawker Siddeley in 1959 required the firms to explore the possibility of collaboration with French and American manufacturers; and BAC's design study contract in 1960 required that these possibilities should be studied further. Encouraged by Mr Duncan Sandys, Minister of Aviation, BAC had discussions with US, French and German manufacturers in 1960–61. The Americans were not interested in a Mach. 2 machine; they believed that a better line to an SST was to use the experience gained with the Mach. 3 B70 bomber. The British believed that Mach. 3 was too difficult, for technical reasons referred to in Chapter Three. The Germans were apparently not interested.

The details of the various cavortings during 1960–61, which led eventually to the Anglo-French Concorde Agreement of November 1962, need not concern us here.[9] It is clear that there were exhaustive discussions, arguments and disagreements. There were basic differences of opinion about the range that should be aimed for – the French favoured the medium range; the British insisted on long range. The French hoped that if a medium range aircraft was developed, this would induce the Americans to aim only for the long range SST market. The British found this argument incomprehensible: if the Americans built a long range SST they could easily adapt it to provide a medium range version. (To adapt a medium-range machine to long range capability is very much more difficult.) Arguments about range and about design continued long after the agreement was signed.

The Anglo-French Concorde Agreement to develop an SST was signed on 29th November, 1962. The cost of research and development was estimated at £150m to £170m. There was no clause allowing for cancellation or for the

9. They are narrated in some detail in *The Concorde Affair*.

withdrawal of either partner prior to the end of the development stage. No limit on costs was specified – nor was there provision for review if the costs passed a certain level.

The money was to be provided entirely by the governments – there was no provision, as there was incorporated in the US SST project, for the manufacturers themselves to provide a small percentage of the capital. If such a clause – for perhaps 10 per cent to be contributed by the manufacturers – had been included it seems certain that the cost estimates would have been more realistic. But it may be doubtful whether, under any such terms, the manufacturers would have been willing (let alone enthusiastic) to embark upon the project.

Subsequent developments, and the prodigious increases in the cost of this project from which the partners had provided themselves with no means of withdrawal, are described in Chapter 8: *The Cost of Concorde*.

CHAPTER THREE

SST Design

Aluminium or Titanium? – A Crucial Choice

The most important choice an SST designer can make is the choice of metal to be used in the aircraft's exterior. Aluminium and titanium are the two main contenders. The choice strongly influences the design of the plane – and determines the upper limit on cruising speed.

Aluminium (atomic number 13) has low tensile strength and a low melting temperature (660°C). An aluminium plane cannot be permitted to fly faster than about 1,400 or 1,500 mph because at higher speeds the frontal portions could become so hot as to soften significantly, and dangers from excessive strain and metal fatigue could arise. The attraction of aluminium is that it is cheap, and satisfactory methods of fabricating it are well established.

Titanium (atomic number 22) is exceedingly strong. It has high tensile strength, high softening temperature, and high melting temperature (1,800°C). Thus a titanium aircraft wing can withstand the severe heating that results when the plane knifes through the air at 1,800 mph. Methods of fabricating structures of titanium were almost unknown a few years ago, but much research has been done on this subject in recent years; see, for example, the May 1968 *Aerospace Technology*.

The Anglo-French designers chose aluminium – to save time and money. They could start design and construction almost immediately, using a readily available material and standard fabrication techniques. They accepted the fact that their plane could not be permitted to fly faster than about 1,500 mph. The particular aluminium alloy chosen was

Hiduminium RR58, which withstands higher temperature than pure aluminium does.

The Soviet designers likewise chose aluminium and accepted the resulting limitation on speed. However, they employed titanium in certain crucial portions of the frontal surfaces.

Boeing engineers, doing their design work some years later, specified titanium in order that their SST would be able to withstand temperatures produced by an 1,800 mph airstream. Staggering problems were presented: new sources of titanium metal would be needed and new methods of fabricating it into intricate structures would be required. Long series of tests would be necessary to show what strength and durability had been achieved. Novel problems in corrosion were encountered. But the designers held out for the 1,800 mph speed – and titanium. Indeed, strong arguments can be made that if an SST is to be built at all, it should be a very fast one: to accept all the obstacles and costs entailed in supersonic flight merely for a *small* increase in speed would be eminently unwise.

Anglo-French Concorde SST

History

As we have seen, an agreement between the British and French governments to embark on a joint programme of designing and building two models of a Concorde SST was signed in November 1962, with the expectation that the cost of the programme would be £150–170m.

By 1967 construction was well under way. The British effort was concentrated at the British Aircraft Corporation (BAC) of Bristol, England. The French effort was managed by Sud-Aviation of Toulouse, France.

The first prototype, called Concorde-001, was assembled at Toulouse. Roll-out was on 1st September, 1968. The first (low speed) flight was on 2nd March, 1969, and the first supersonic flight was on 1st October, 1969. The second prototype, Concorde-002, was assembled at Bristol; the first flight was on 9th April, 1969.

Work was also proceeding on six production models – even before the high-speed test-flying programme had been commenced.

Design

The Concorde is a highly streamlined mid-wing monoplane with a fixed triangular (delta-shaped) wing and four engines mounted at the rear. The nose is hinged, and droops for improved pilot visibility during landing. Other specifications are:

Length, width, height: 193 ft, 84 ft, 38 ft.
Weight at take-off, fully loaded: 367,000 lb (164 tons).
Maximum fuel load: 24,000 gallons (almost 90 tons).
Engines: four Bristol-SNECMA Olympus 593 engines of 350,000 lb thrust each, using afterburners.[1]
Take-off speed: 227 mph (almost twice that of many existing planes).
Take-off distance: 10,900 ft (more than two miles).
Cruising speed and altitude: Mach. 2.0 (about 1,400 mph) at 55,000 ft.
Number of passengers: 100 to 132.
Range with full load: 4,000 statute miles.
Take-off noise, landing noise: substantially greater than for today's commercial planes.
Sonic boom overpressure: about 2.0 lb/sq. ft. Bang-zone extends entire length of supersonic flightpath and is about 40 miles wide.
Speed at approach to landing: 180 mph, with 10.8 degree upward tilt.

Technical difficulties and alterations

Even before the Concorde's subsonic test-flights were completed, several shortcomings of the design became apparent. In the spring of 1968 Sir George Edwards, Managing Director of BAC, said that there was concern about rudder flutter problems and excessive temperature in the nacelles

1. 'Afterburning' involves the injection of extra fuel into the jet pipe, to produce more thrust.

during reverse thrust of the engines. Difficulties were encountered also with the plane's droop nose, the highly complex system of fuel transfer for in-flight trim, and the brakes. Early in 1969 Mr Anthony Wedgwood Benn, British Minister of Technology, announced in Parliament that the two pre-production models of the Concorde were to be modified in many ways, including: changing the shape of leading edges of wing, wing tips, and extreme end of fuselage; increasing the fuel capacity; and considerably modifying the engines. The pre-production models are to be 25 tons heavier and 9 ft longer than the prototypes, according to *Aviation Week* of 3rd February, 1969; see also the October 1969 *Congressional Hearings.*

On 5th January, 1970, Arthur Reed reported in *The Times* that 3,500 separate engineering modifications were being made to prototype 002 at Bristol – modifications that had been found to be necessary during the trial of 001 in France. Modifications to the flying controls had involved delving deep into the aircraft's structure.

Flight International, of 21st May, 1970, disclosed what the modifications to the flying controls were all about. It appears that at supersonic speeds the aircraft tended to get out of control. 'Pilot-induced oscillations', 'tendency to divergence', 'proverse yaw effect' were referred to; these appear to mean that the pilot was unable to control the aircraft because when he tried to make course corrections the effect achieved was the opposite of that intended: the aircraft went further off course.

Schedule

Subsonic test flights on the two prototypes continued throughout 1969. Test flights at supersonic speed started late in 1969, with the French prototype. Also, late in 1969, a route for supersonic test flying of the 002 prototype down the Irish Sea, mostly over the sea but crossing western Scotland and Northern Ireland, West Wales, and Cornwall, was disclosed. Flights on this route were scheduled to commence in December 1969, but as a result of technical delays they did not start until 1st September, 1970, and continued

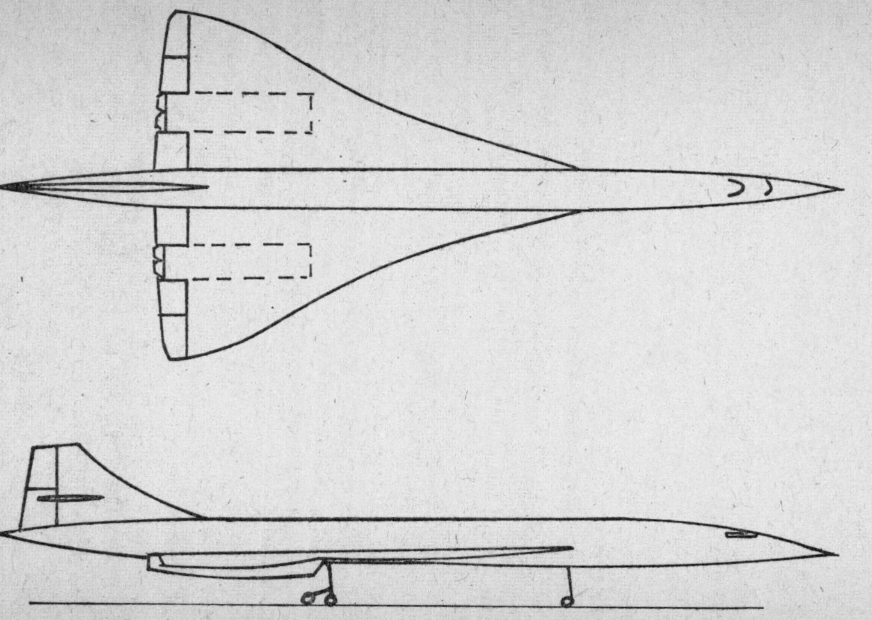

Fig. 1. Silhouette of Concorde

throughout October down the Western corridor. Testing is scheduled to continue for three years, but the manufacturers hope to be able to prove early in the programme that the Concorde meets its design specifications.

Soviet Tu-144 SST

The Soviet Tu-144 SST, built at the Tupolev plant at Shukovsky near Moscow and named after its designer, Andrei N. Tupolev, has a fixed, swept-back, delta-shaped wing much like that of the Concorde. Here too the principal metal used is an aluminium alloy, with some use of titanium also, and the plane's speed must be limited to about 1,500 mph. The windows are 8 inches in diameter.

The plane is smaller than the Concorde and would carry fewer passengers: about 98 to 120, with three hostesses and a crew of three. Maximum loaded weight is 330,000 lb. The plane is powered by four Kuznetsov NK-144 two-shaft turbofan engines mounted in pairs in two nacelles beneath the fuselage centreline. Each engine provides 18,600 lb thrust during normal operation and 38,500 lb when the afterburners are in use.

Recent design modifications include greater camber of wingtips and a slight widening of the forward part of the wing in order to improve performance at the lower end of the speed range. Other characteristics are: length 186 feet, wingspan 72 ft, operational ceiling 65,000 ft. The sonic bang overpressure is said to be similar to that of the Concorde.

The first (subsonic) flight was on 31st December, 1968, and the first supersonic flight was on 5th June, 1969. The fact that the Tupolev's first subsonic flight was some months before the Concorde's was regarded as something of a propaganda victory. But Western aviation commentators generally have not regarded the Russian SST as a serious challenge. They point out that no Russian aircraft has yet penetrated the western market, and that the Russians have no world-wide back-up system for after-sales servicing.

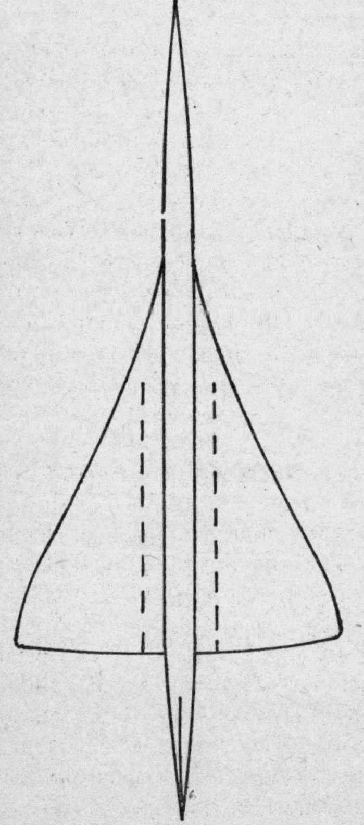

Fig 2. TU 144 in proportion

Boeing B-2707-300 SST

History

The history of the Boeing SST project is one of repeated failures. Three separate stages may be discerned.

The first stage (1960–64) began with the Congressional hearings of May 1960 by the House Committee on Science and Astronautics. Believing that the development of an SST would be reasonably economical and told by the promoters that the sonic bang problem would not be serious, Congress provided, in August 1961, $11m for the first year of a two-year research programme. In January 1963 President John F. Kennedy created a cabinet-level coordinating committee, and the National Aeronautics and Space Administration (NASA) awarded short-term design-study contracts to Boeing and Lockheed. Airframe and systems-study contracts were awarded in April, and on 3rd June the President announced his decision to proceed with an SST design and construction programme. (He promised that 'In no event will the Government investment be permitted to exceed $750m', according to the *Congressional Record* of 31st October, 1969.)

In July and August of 1963 requests for proposals as to components and system designs were issued. In November Congress voted $60m for a Fiscal Year 1964 budget for SST design. In January 1964 three airframe manufacturers and three engine manufacturers submitted preliminary design proposals. SST advocates were hopeful that SSTs might be in commercial use by 1968. But in April 1964 President Lyndon B. Johnson announced that none of the designs was satisfactory. Four years had passed, and still no satisfactory design existed.

The second stage (1964–8) was more dramatically unsuccessful. In May 1964 the President called for contracts for further design proposals, and in June the Government arranged six-month contracts with Boeing and Lockheed (for airframe design) and General Electric and Pratt & Whitney (for engine design). In July 1965 the President announced an 18-month extension of this work and indicated that $140m would be requested for Fiscal Year 1966. On 31st December, 1966, the Government announced its decision in favour of the Boeing swing-wing airframe design and the General Electric engine. '... climaxing three-and-one-half years of intense competition' (*Fortune*, February 1967). In 1967 and 1968 the Federal Aviation Administration announced that the Boeing swing-wing design was excellent and that the manufacturer was essentially ready to 'start cutting metal'. On 21st October, 1968, Boeing announced the abandonment of the swing-wing design.

What was the ill-fated B-2707-200 swing-wing design? It featured wings that were mounted on gigantic hinges, or bearings. The wings were to be extended (i.e. swung almost straight out to the sides) for take-off and landing or other low-speed flight in order to provide maximum lift. They were to be swung backwards and inwards, close to the fuselage, for high-speed flight, to reduce the frontal area, reduce drag, and reduce the intensity of sonic bang. With wings extended for take-off, the width of the plane was 180 ft; the length was 318 ft. Loaded with 50,000 gallons (almost 200 tons) of fuel and 330 passengers, the plane had a gross take-off weight of 670,000 lb, or 335 tons. The weight of the empty plane was 350,000 lb. Cruising speed was 1,800 mph at 65,000 ft. Range was expected to be 4,000 miles (until more accurate estimates showed the range would be drastically less, and the design was abandoned). No adequate statement has been provided by the FAA[1] as to why the impracticability of the swing-wing design had not been appreciated earlier.

The third stage (1968 to date) was begun in great agony for Boeing Co. As explained in detail in the October 1968 *Fortune*, Boeing engineers had for months sought frantically for a successful design that could be announced before the failure of the swing-wing design became generally known. Some Boeing engineers clung to the hope that the swing-wing design might yet be improved and made accept-

1. Federal Aviation Administration.

able; but Boeing's main effort was to find an alternative – quickly.

On 21st October, 1968, Boeing made its announcement: 'The Boeing Company formally announced ... that it had abandoned its swing-wing design for the US supersonic airliner in favour of a relatively conventional fixed-wing plane' (*New York Times,* 22nd October, 1968). The new design, called B-2707-300, was submitted to the FAA on 15th January, 1969, in not-fully-complete form.

It was to have a 40 per cent more severe sonic bang than the earlier version. The passenger capacity of the new design was less, the take-off speed was much greater, and the expected date of first use was put off four years – until 1978. Lacking the glamorous swing-wing, and with a clear resemblance to the Concorde design and to the rejected Lockheed design of 1966, the new design had sharply reduced popular appeal.

On September 23rd, 1969, President Nixon announced his decision to continue with the development of the SST. This decision was contrary to the recommendations of most of the members of the President's SST Review Committee. (Please see Appendix 2.)

New Design

The detailed design of the Boeing B-2707-300 SST has not been published by the FAA, but many of the main design features are now known, for example from the October 1969 *Congressional Hearings* ref. 94 and recent issues of technical journals on aeronautics. As indicated in Figure 3, the plane would have a fixed wing, of triangular (delta) shape, swept back at 50° – less sharply than in the Concorde. There is an independent horizontal tail. The four engines, mounted independently beneath the wings, are similar to those planned for the earlier design: four GE-4 afterburning turbojet engines of 60,000 to 67,800 lb thrust each. Other characteristics of the engines are: 633 lb/sec airflow; 2,000°F turbine inlet temperature; 308-inch length: 89½-inch maximum diameter; 11,300 lb weight (per General Electric Co. brochure AEC-240R-6/68.)

Other specifications are:

Length, width, and height: 298 ft, 143 ft, 52 ft.

Weight at take-off, fully loaded: 750,000 lb (375 tons).

Fuel: 50,000 gal. (almost 200 tons) of commercial kerosene.

Take-off speed: 220 mph (much faster than today's commercial planes).

Take-off distance: 10,300 ft (almost two miles).

Cruising speed and altitude: 1,800 mph (Mach. 2.7) at 65,000 ft.

Number of passengers: 298.

Range with full load: 4,000 statute miles.

Take-off noise: expected to be greater than for present-day jets: a major problem. Use of afterburning engines makes extremely high noise levels inevitable.

Sonic boom overpressure: 3.5 psf during climb after reaching Mach. 1, and 2.1 during cruise, i.e. about 40 per cent greater than for the abandoned swing-wing design.

Speed on approach to landing: 178 mph (with 10.1° upward tilt).

Technical Difficulties

The story of the technical difficulties encountered in designing the Boeing SST is a long one. The reader is referred to the detailed accounts in *Fortune* ref. 65 and in October 1969 *Congressional Hearings* ref. 94. Major problems were countered in connexion with rigidity, stability, weight, range, engine noise, sonic bang, fuel leak, lightning and fire danger. Many of the problems have not yet been solved.

Schedule

SST proponents have claimed that if all of the pressing problems are solved promptly a first prototype of Boeing SST could be ready for trial flight in 1972, and if no serious difficulty then shows up and adequate (multi-billion-dollar) financing materializes, production planes could be in use by 1978. As a result of the Senate decisions of early December 1970, the future of the project is very seriously in doubt.

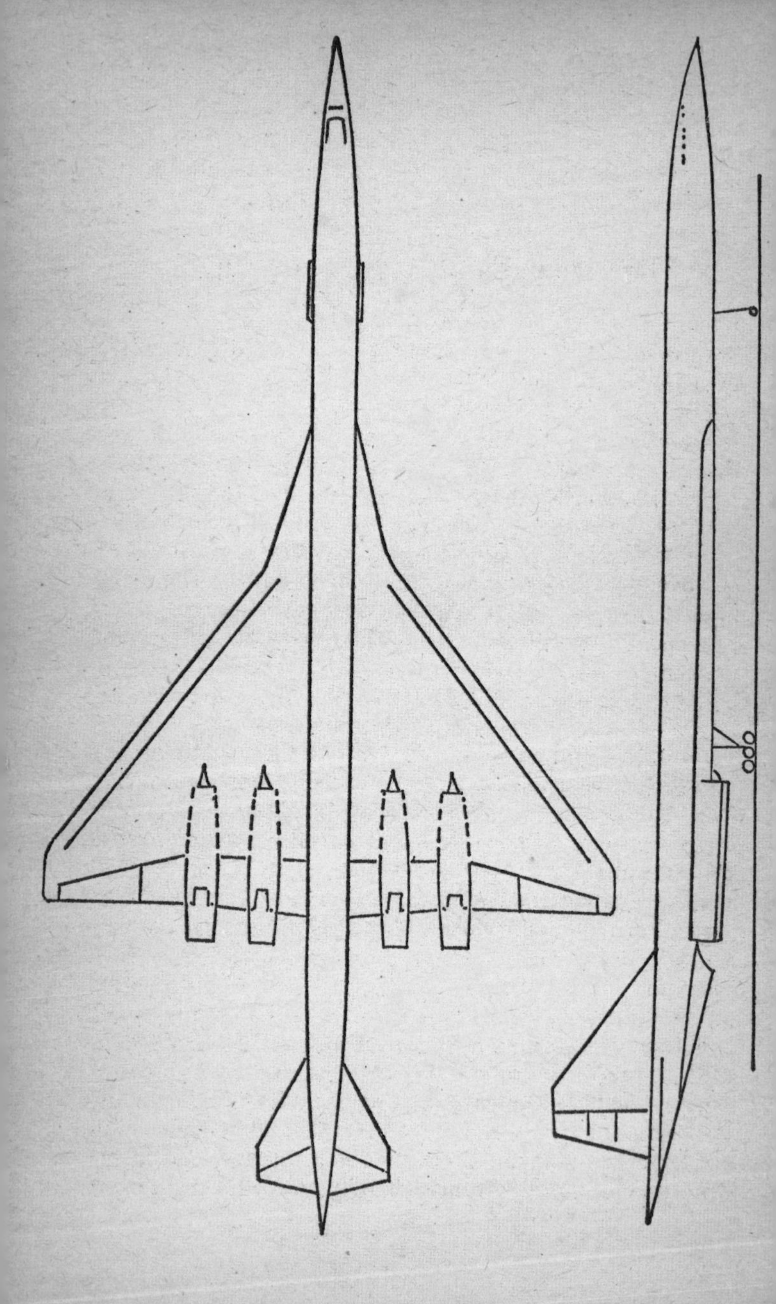

CHAPTER FOUR

The Hazards of Supersonic Flight

Air travel, in the public mind, is undoubtedly associated with the possibility of disaster. To a great extent, this is unfair. The accident record of world civil aviation is very favourable, and the 'disaster' image is fostered by the fact that the occasional crash invariably makes the headlines, while the thousands of safe, successful flights go unremarked. There is no doubt that the number of air crashes could be reduced, if sufficient priority were given to this requirement. Increased safety seems such an obvious priority, of such obvious benefit to airline operators, insurers, crews, passengers, people on the ground; to the image and profitability of civil aviation generally, that it may be wondered why so much less priority has been given to producing increased safety than to producing increased speed.

As long ago as 1961, Mr B. K. O. Lundberg was urging that the priorities be got right – and emphasizing that SST development would inevitably result in distortion of these priorities. It does this in two ways: by consuming vast amounts of money and skilled effort, some of which could have been used on improving safety; and also by taking passengers into a 'regime' which is, inherently, more dangerous – which would remain more dangerous even after long experience, and which is certainly more dangerous in the initial stages.

Apart from the greater dangers that are inherent in supersonic transport in general, there are certain special areas of danger. The SST will carry a far greater fuel load than any earlier type of air transport. The full operational fuel load of the Concorde at take-off will be about 90 tons; that of the Boeing SST, almost 200 tons. These quantities of fuel *exceed* the weight of the empty aircraft. At take-off, an SST is a veritable flying fuel tank.

Much of the fuel will be stored in the wings. Many different tanks will be used; the tanks are to be interconnected by large numbers of pipes, valves, and an elaborate system of pumps for transferring fuel from one tank to another, to maintain balance of the plane. The leading edges of the wings will become very hot – about 500 or even 600°F in some instances (ref. 109, p. 108).

A greater wealth of material concerning the anticipated dangers facing SSTs is available in the United States than is commonly circulated in Britain. The Federal Aviation Administration's worries as to fire hazards are evident in its 200-page 'Tentative Airworthiness Standards for Supersonic Transports', January 1969 (ref. 102). On page 99 one finds:

> 'A broader safety problem exists, arising from the presence of ignitable fuel-air mixtures in the tanks and venting systems. Possible sources of ignition are: electrostatic discharges, unusual lightning strikes, ground fires, unforeseen arcing and sparking from electrical components, and hot metal fragments from engine disintegration. This potential fire and explosion hazard is not unique to the SST; however, it represents a safety threat which is more critical for the SST because of the broad fuel temperature ranges likely to be experienced, and the greater quantities of fuel stored in or near the fuselage areas.'

On page 104 the danger of fire in empty spaces between fuel tanks is discussed:

> 'Spaces may exist, for instance, in the leading edges of wings where high temperatures will prevail as a result of aerodynamic heating. Spaces may exist under fuselage tanks if the tanks are elevated to protect them from possible damage during a wheels-up landing. In the event of such a landing, scraping action would produce both heat and sparks. Other sources of ignition could originate

from equipment located in the space or from punctures in the skin where temperatures up to the stagnation temperature might occur. It is extremely difficult to prevent all leaks . . . fuel leakage into areas surrounding fuel storage is frequently encountered in service.'

Engine fires, too, are a threat. On pages 121 and 122 we read:

'The capability to shut off the flow of flammable fluids will be even more important in the case of the SST because an engine fire occurring during high-Mach. flight will be difficult, if not impossible, to extinguish with extinguishing agent. Engine and cowl surfaces at these high speeds will re-ignite a fire if flow continues.

In the supersonic aircraft, there may be a need for protection not only against burn-through but against radiation effects which may be of sufficient magnitude to affect other parts of the aircraft or to initiate fires on the protected side of the firewall . . .'

Hail

Subsonic planes, travelling at 300 to 500 mph, have been seriously damaged on encountering hailstones one or two inches in diameter, as indicated in many technical reports (for example, World Meteorological Organization *Technical Note 89*) (ref. 109). For an SST to enter a region of hail is far more serious because of the greater speed of the plane; the velocity of the hailstones relative to the aircraft is far greater than the speed of an ordinary .22-rifle bullet. The SST flies very high, but hail is occasionally present at altitudes greater than 65,000 ft (ref. 28, p. 80).

The FAA's worries concerning hail have been stated clearly enough (ref. 102, pp. 177, 178). Discussing possibilities of SSTs colliding with birds and hailstones, FAA engineers stated:

'The most critical of such materials at supersonic speeds

is likely to be hailstones. A review of meteorological literature on hailstone observations and theory of development indicates that little reliable information is available concerning what sizes and densities can be expected in the high altitudes. One difficulty is that of determining hail size in the air. There is ample evidence that hailstones occur at high altitudes, with convective cloud tops up to 70,000 ft. Over an eight-year period, USAF aircraft are reported to have experienced 272 damaging hail encounters. Forty-six per cent of these encounters occurred above 20,000 ft, with maximum height at 44,000 ft. Pilots have reported hailstones of possibly three to five inches between 29,000 and 37,000 ft.

At the October 1967 FAA Industry meeting, it was commented that strikes are being reported in spite of weather radar and that we should test larger hail sizes, up to five inches ... FAA feels that testing with fewer than actual concentrations will establish the strength to resist impact, as multiple strikes at the same spot are unlikely ... For engines it is felt that minor damage from two-inch stones would be acceptable.'

The FAA has called for sufficient tests '... to assure that (1) encounter of large size (e.g. 4-inch diameter) hail, and (2) encounter of hail at higher speeds (e.g. speed associated with 50,000 ft cruise Mach. number) will not result in catastrophic structural failure.'

Lightning

It is suggested by recent researches[1] conducted into the susceptibility of various metals to lightning, that the titanium Boeing SST would be more at risk than the aluminium Concorde. The cruising altitude of both planes is such that they would be high above most lightning storms.

1. 'Aviation Week' 13th November, 1967, commenting on the work of the lightning and transient Research Institute in the USA

Clear air turbulence

When a subsonic plane enters a region in which a sudden upward stream of air is encountered, or a sequence of upward and downward streams occurs, the sudden forces on the wings are enormous. The wings may bend by a foot or two (measured at the tips), and the plane may temporarily find itself in a dive or climb.

The US national Transportation Safety Board, after turbulence had resulted in the crash of an airliner in Nebraska in 1966, concluded that turbulence 'may be more critical today than in the past' because of higher speeds and other factors (*Aviation Daily*, 16th May, 1968)

Some turbulent regions may be seen well ahead of time by the pilot, and he may be able to detour around them. But some severe turbulence occurs in clear air ('clear air turbulence', or CAT), and the plane may plunge into such a region without warning. At altitudes of about 55,000 to 65,000 ft, where SSTs will cruise, CAT regions have been found to be surprisingly numerous, according to investigations made with military supersonic planes. XB-70 pilots have found turbulence in 7.2 per cent of the over-USA mileage flown at 40,000 to 60,000 ft altitude, and in 3.3 per cent of the mileage over 65,000 ft. (Report NASA-TN-D-4209.)

SSTs, with their exceptionally high speed, are especially vulnerable to sudden accelerations and strains from CAT. Many pages are devoted to the subject in a recent World Meteorological Organization report (ref. 19). The higher speed of the SST, the thinner profiles of the wings, the poor visibility, and poor manoeuvrability all conspire to make CAT a major threat.

Poor visibility and poor manoeuvrability

Travelling at 1,400 mph, a Concorde covers a mile in three seconds; ten miles in 30 seconds. At 1,800 mph, a Boeing SST would travel a mile in two seconds. If atmospheric conditions limit a pilot's vision to less than ten miles, he can see no further ahead than the distance to be travelled in the next 20 or 30 seconds. With the retractable nose of the SST raised, and the 'visor' in position for supersonic flight, the pilot's visibility is poor.

The human reaction time of the pilot, and the time taken for the large and heavy SST to respond to his signals, are such that sudden avoidance of a visible obstacle is unlikely to be possible.[2]

To bank the aircraft and make a slight turn must take some seconds, and in that time it will have travelled many miles.

Dodging thunderstorms or regions of hail or turbulence many miles ahead may also be impossible. Even if the pilot's reaction time and the responsiveness of the machine allowed sudden evasive manoeuvres, such change of direction might impose upon the passengers acceleration forces far beyond anything previously experienced by air passengers. Military pilots of supersonic aircraft and crews of space rockets experience large acceleration forces, many times the force of gravity – but these men are trained to the experience, they are all in excellent health, and they are strapped into their seats or harnesses.

Even at subsonic speeds poor visibility and poor manoeuvrability create problems. When, in June 1969, the occasion of the Queen's birthday was utilized for a Concorde publicity-promotion stunt, and prototype 002 flew along the Mall in London, the impossibility of the pilot seeing the ground necessitated the Concorde being led by an RAF aircraft, which acted as a guide. In the crowded airspace near airfields, hundreds of near misses or 'air misses' occur each year. Occasionally fatal collisions occur; quite often disaster is narrowly avoided by very rapid evasive action by pilots.

One of the most dramatic air crashes ever – that of the unique, 250-ton bomber XB70, piloted by Al White, on 8th June, 1966 – was blamed upon the poor visibility available to the pilot. The crash was described in detail in *Life* of

2. The diameter of the turning circle at supersonic speeds is about 100 miles.

11th November, 1966, and the February 1967 *Reader's Digest*: 'With limited vision from inside the XB-70's long, reptilian nose, White could not watch the other planes . . .' A photographic plane collided gently with the XB-70, then '. . . pitched upward, rolled sharply to the left and somersaulted . . . slicing the big plane's two vertical fins.'

Air Conditioning and Pressurization

In a subsonic plane, if cabin pressure is lost while at moderate altitude, crew and passengers don oxygen masks and suffer no harm. But in an SST, the situation is quite different: the altitude is so great (about 65,000 ft), and the outside air pressure there is so low, that should the plane lose its pressure, sudden 'boiling of the blood' would occur, producing unconsciousness of crew and passengers within about one minute. Oxygen masks would not avail; a disastrous crash would be unavoidable. Loss of pressure would occur, for example, if several windows of the plane were to be blown out, or a small bomb blew a hole a few feet in diameter in the side of the plane. The air-pressure-maintenance system is designed to maintain at least a barely livable pressure if a *small* opening (one-foot diameter or less) occurs in the side of the plane, e.g. if one small window is blown (ref. 94, p. 121).

The special requirements of air-conditioning and pressurization at supersonic speeds and at 60,000 ft necessitate the provision of special systems. Prospective supersonic travellers may be interested to know some of the details of the elaborate apparatus upon whose constant efficiency their lives would depend.

'The air for this system is obtained by tapping the engine compressors. Unfortunately, in this case, this air leaves the engines at a temperature of about 600°C, so before it reaches the cabin each of the four streams is passed through a primary heat exchanger, a secondary heat exchanger, a fuel heat exchanger and a cold air unit. Of course this makes complications and weight, but at 60,000 ft there just is not enough air for Concorde to simply scoop up all it needs for the cabins. To keep the crew and passengers in safety and comfort all the air in the cabins must be changed every two minutes, which involves shifting approximately 5,000 cubic ft of air in this time.

'In the primary heat exchanger the hot air is cooled to about 200°C by ambient air taken from outside the aircraft, used and discharged overboard. It will probably receive a second treatment at the same time, in that the nickel in the structure of the primary heat exchanger will act as a catalytic cracker to cause the undesirably high quantity of ozone in the cabin air to dissociate into normal oxygen. At 60,000 ft the ozone content of air is high and if the crew are not to be troubled by conjunctivitis and other irritations this ozone must be reduced by a factor of 100. The passengers would probably not be affected even if nothing were done about the ozone because they do not spend long enough at very high altitudes.

'From the primary heat exchanger the air will flow through a radioactive particle filter and into the compressor of the cold air unit, which consists of a turbine and a radial compressor turning at some 60,000 rev/min. This raises the temperature of the air again but raises its pressure, so that expansion through the turbine can be used to reduce its temperature sharply. But even this sudden expansion would not give the outlet temperature required (about –25°C) if the air were allowed to pass straight from the compressor to the turbine. So to cool it again it is put through the secondary heat exchanger and the fuel heat exchanger. The former is another air to air unit in which ambient air is used and discharged overboard and the cabin air temperature is reduced from 310 to 200°C approximately. In the latter, engine fuel is used as the cooling medium and the air temperature is brought down to about 90°C, at which it can be allowed into the turbine to emerge at about –25°C.

'On its way to the cabin from the turbine outlet the air is led through a water separator and a non-return valve fitted at the point of entry into the manifold in the pressure floor of the cabin. There is also a temperature control valve connected between the compressor inlet and the turbine outlet so that cold air may be mixed with warm air bled from the upstream side of the cold air unit, for the system has to heat the cabin during subsonic flight in addition to cooling it during supersonic flight. For the same reason, and to allow for the variety of ambient conditions an aircraft encounters, there are by-passes across the heat exchangers which can be opened if necessary.

'From the manifold, which connects the four subsystems, risers within the cabin wall take the air to the main distribution ducts which run the length of the cabin above the hat racks. The majority of the air actually enters the cabin through adjustable punkahs in the service panels, but some enters at the inner surface of the windows to reduce the effects of radiation. The discharge ducts are at floor level along each side of the cabin and centrally in the roof.

'The air conditioning and pressurization system is applied to the whole of the fuselage between the pressure bulkheads and above the pressure floor, also to the forward baggage hold and forward systems bay which are below the pressure floor level. Some of the air discharged from the cabin is used to cool the landing gear bays and the after systems bay; the roof discharge air is circulated around the cabin walls, within the insulation, to assist in cooling the structure. A maximum pressure differential equivalent to a cabin altitude of 6,000 ft at a real altitude of 60,000 ft is maintained, controlled normally by an electro-pneumatic discharge/relief valve (in the rear fuselage section) which is part of an automatic control system for temperature and pressure. There is a manual system also, with a separate discharge/relief valve, and a ground connexion located in the centre section.'[3]

Cosmic Radiation

It is not yet known whether intense solar flares from the sun would occur often enough to create a serious problem from high-energy ionizing radiation. According to an article,

3. From *Concorde – the story, the facts, the figures* – T. E. Blackall, Foulis, Henley-on-Thames, Oxfordshire, pp. 65 and 67.

'Radiobiological Aspects of the Supersonic Transport',[4] (ref. 42) ionization from cosmic radiation is at a maximum at altitudes of the order of 60,000 to 80,000 ft. The ambient radiation here consists mainly of charged particles (protons, alpha particles, etc.) of very high energy, i.e. many millions of electron volts. A single such particle can do lasting damage to a gene of a human cell. The skin of the plane is not a protection, but just the reverse: it actually causes multiplication of the damaging particles by the process of *shower production* – i.e. one particle passing through the material of the aircraft generates a 'shower' of further particles.

The radiation levels inside the cabins of SSTs at cruising altitudes are of the order of 100 times their value at sea-level, and amount to 1 or 2 millirems per hour. The usual limit on dose allowed to the public is 500 millirems *per year*, and a limit of 2 millirems per hour is commonly imposed. In the absence of solar flares, the actual level in the SST cabin will usually be just below this limit.

The harmfulness of the cosmic radiation is difficult to predict from laboratory experiments. The cosmic-ray spectrum cannot be duplicated in the laboratory, adequate experimentation on human beings is prohibited, and genetic damage might take decades, or generations, to appear.

It is generally agreed that a dose of such radiation equivalent to 500 rems may well prove fatal. The chance that a solar flare might produce a dose of the order of 1 to 20 rems cannot at present be ruled out. Governmental regulations are such that if an SST at high altitude were to receive a dose of 15 rems or more, the pilots and passengers would be advised not to risk receiving additional doses in that year, i.e. advised not to participate in high-altitude SST flights for many months. The economic waste of grounding an SST pilot, whose training for SST flight represents a considerable financial investment, is obvious (ref. 41).

It is well established that any high-energy radiation that is unnecessary should be avoided. This is true of all persons,

4. Report of the International Commission on Radio biological protection 1966.

and is especially true of pregnant women. The human foetus, particularly during the first few weeks of pregnancy when that condition is usually not known, can be seriously damaged by a very small dose of radiation; even a 1 rem dose presents an appreciable risk. It has therefore been suggested that women of child-bearing age might be advised to avoid such high-altitude flights. SST hostesses, likewise, should be beyond childbearing age, and all crew members should be classified as 'radiation workers', with their doses and flight-hours controlled accordingly.

Dr S. R. Mohler, Chief, FAA Aeromedical Applications Division, has indicated that SST crews would run the risk that radiation '. . . may shorten the life span by 5 to 10 per cent and the gross signs of ageing may appear earlier than would otherwise be anticipated.' Other possible results of exposure to radiation, according to Dr Mohler, are damage to sperm cells, bone marrow, lung tissues, kidney tissues, and the lymphatic system – and leukaemia. (See also *Astronautics and Aeronautics*, September 1964.)

A pilot could avoid most of the radiation from a solar flare if he were to dive the plane quickly to much lower altitude. The hazards of such an unannounced dive into perhaps already crowded airspace are sufficient to rule out such action (refs. 42, 109, 64, 83).

Ozone danger

Special precautions must be taken to eliminate active ozone from the cabin of the SSTs. Ozone exists naturally at high altitude, and it is now known that even extremely small concentrations (of the order of one part per million) are dangerous (109).

According to the FAA: 'Atmospheric ozone concentrations at SST cruising altitudes are several times greater than the maximum permissible cabin ozone concentrations . . . Ozone contamination following system malfunctions may be an added hazard concerning SST cabin environmental control' (102).

Metal Fatigue at High Temperature

The early British Comet planes suffered disasters because of metal fatigue. In the SSTs, fatigue is especially troublesome because of the extreme flexibility of the structures, the enormous forces produced when flying through bumpy air, and the fact that some of the metal parts are at very high temperature (from the impacting supersonic airflow). Also, big temperature differentials exist: some parts very hot, near-by parts cold, with resulting thermal-expansion strains superimposed on other kinds of strain. During the course of every flight the aircraft is subjected to very great, and very rapid, changes in temperature. At the beginning of the flight it is at the temperature prevailing at ground level. It climbs rapidly during subsonic flight, through levels at which subsonic aircraft operate – and where flying conditions are icy cold. Within minutes the machine reaches supersonic speed, and its outer parts become hot – in parts, very hot.

It is impossible to make adequate laboratory studies on such combinations of sudden flexures and high and non-uniform temperatures; thousands of hours of actual flight through turbulent air – even several years of testing – would be necessary to provide assurance that metal fatigue, shortened useful life, and perhaps sudden disaster will not occur. Because drastically new metal fabrication methods and new structural arrangements are used, practical experience is, at this stage, meagre. It is already well known that the aluminium alloy Hiduminium RR58 used in the Concorde '... gradually loses its strength from the cumulative effects of heating' (*New Scientist*, 9th May, 1968, p. 285). See also *Aerospace Technology*, 20th May, 1968.

The FAA has stated that '... it is extremely difficult to assure that fatigue cracking of the (SST) structure will not occur in service or to predict where it will occur.' Also '... landing and take-off loading conditions may be critical for significant portions of SST flight structure such as the fuselage. Failure of such structure during these high speed ground conditions could be catastrophic' (ref. 102, pp 65, 66).

High Landing Speed

The most dangerous part of flying is the landing, and the actual landing speed is an important factor. Experience with many kinds of planes has shown that, other things being comparable, the hazard increases with the 3rd power of the landing speed. Thus, increasing the landing speed by 50 per cent may be expected to increase the hazard by a factor of roughly $(1.50)^3$ or about 3.4.

The SSTs are to have very high landing speeds (about 180 mph) and the landing operation is expected to be particularly hazardous (*Aeroplane*, 6th December, 1967).

Inability to 'Hold' for Long Periods – incompatibility with other kinds of planes

Subsonic planes, using relatively little fuel per hour, can hold for hours near a crowded airport, awaiting permission to land. If the chosen airport is closed because of a storm or an accident, the subsonic plane can fly to another airport, perhaps 500 or 1,000 miles away, if necessary. But the SST uses in the order of a half ton of fuel per minute, and can ill afford to take off with any greater reserve of fuel than is absolutely necessary. Thus its ability to hold over an airport, or to be diverted to a distant airport, is restricted. The Concorde's fuel reserve guaranteed by the manufacturer – for flight from Paris to New York – is only '. . . 30 minutes over alternate' and '. . . this appears unrealistic' because of the need to hold during congestion at peak load times (*Aeroplane*, 17th April, 1968).

> 'In the early days, there were ideas that the supersonic aircraft would have priority on routes, that it would sweep through like an express train while slower traffic was shunted out of the way. This would have meant that reserve fuel only needed to be provided for bad weather at destination. This idea was soon discarded: the air traffic system is at its most efficient when it deals with an orderly flow of traffic presented in the order of arrival, with

special provision made only for those in distress. Further, why should the supersonic aircraft get special treatment, just because they happen to go faster? Given this, the Concorde would have to join the traffic pattern near airports and manoeuvre within it at a speed which allowed it to match other traffic. This was likely to be a speed less than the most efficient subsonic speed of the Concorde.' (Air Commodore John Davis *The Concorde Affair*, pp. 86–7.)

Mr Davis points out that relative speeds are not the only important factors here; there is also the question of the sizes of turning circles: 'The faster the aircraft goes, the wider the circle it takes to turn. Traffic patterns clearly want aircraft to turn within the prescribed limits.'

With its high speed, high altitude of cruise, poor manoeuvrability, and limited fuel reserves, the SST is in many ways poorly compatible with, or incompatible with, other types of planes, as regards routes, headway separations, holding patterns, landing priorities, and other obvious categories such as pilot training and aircraft servicing. Extra expense and perhaps extra danger may be involved (*Aviation Weekly*, 24th October, 1968, pp. 149 and 153).

As John Davis points out, the necessity for SSTs to operate compatibly with the operating patterns of other aircraft creates further problems in ensuring adequate fuel reserves. How much reserve fuel is essential?

'Reserve requirements set by the various authorities and airlines differ. Some define a given percentage of fuel plus, say, one defined diversion to an alternative airfield: others ask for a lower percentage plus diversion plus defined holding in the circuit. We need not go into details of these: each version has its solid supporting arguments, but to take one example, the difference between the reserve fuel defined by the Federal Aviation Administration in the United States and that defined by one airline comes to no less than 7,000 lb. When one remembers that the payload which was being aimed at was between 20,000 and 25,000 lb, the size of the fuel reserves was obviously vital. But they were in their turn conditioned by the manner in which the airlines would operate the aircraft.'[5]

Limited number of Airports available in emergency

Because SSTs require very long runways and specially strengthened surfaces (to take the enormous weight and landing impact), relatively few airports can accept an SST. Thus the number of secondary, or emergency, landing sites is small.

The problems and dangers inherent in SST should not be exaggerated. But, in addition to the dangers already referred to, several other problematical areas have been defined, which are worthy of consideration.

Pilot Strain

The strain on the SST pilot will be enormous. The number of tasks he must perform, their novelty, and the requisite speed of execution are impressive. Even on conventional transport planes the strain is great. In 1966 there were six instances in which a pilot on duty on the flight deck of a commercial plane suffered sudden incapacitation from cardiovascular disease (*Aviation Daily*, 22nd December, 1967). In the last eight years, 14 commercial transports crashed during training flights. The strain on an SST pilot must be exceptionally great: he is handling a more cumbersome and complicated plane, relying on a greater array of automatic equipment, with need for quicker decisions.

Inadequate Testing

When testing small planes, produced at reasonable cost, a test pilot can put the plane through its paces rigorously. Besides trying out all the recommended flight conditions and manoeuvres, he can try some extra-curricular tests,

5. *The Concorde Affair*, p. 88.

such as flying through bad storms, diving steeply, stalling, landing cross-wind, or deliberately making a hard landing with exaggerated bounce. He can discover whether the plane holds up well even when abused.

But the SST pilot, realizing that the prototype plane may have cost £100m or $250m and that to build a replacement would take a year or two, must be careful not to make the extreme tests which would be of so much interest.

If some design error is found in a small plane, the manufacturer can modify the design quickly and produce and test additional planes. But to modify an SST could be a major undertaking, slowing down the whole programme by months or years and causing large financial loss.

The fact has been illustrated, by experience with the Concorde, which in the autumn and winter of 1969–70 had to be extensively modified. Modifications to the manual back-up flight control mechanism, which had been built deep down in the bottom of the aircraft with many other components on top, proved to be a difficult and time-consuming operation.

Sabotage or Hijack

From time to time aircraft have been sabotaged by persons with a grudge against some passenger, or persons hoping to collect the life-insurance on a certain individual. More recently there have been instances of hijackers endangering the lives of passengers and crew. If, as a result of some such action even a comparatively small hole were blown in an SST, the air pressure would be so drastically reduced that the passengers and crew would be likely to die almost at once.

The radio operator might not survive long enough to send off a message as to the cause of the disaster; thus the cause might forever remain a mystery. In addition to the tragic deaths of passengers and crews, there would be substantial financial loss. Even a single such crash – unexplained – might cause the public to shy away from SSTs, and might cause the regulatory agencies to ground all SSTs pending prolonged inquiry.

CHAPTER FIVE

The Cause of the Sonic Bang

Physical causes of the bang

The 'sonic bang' of a supersonic aircraft is a sudden pressure disturbance, or shock-wave, in the air. The supersonic shock-wave is, in some respects, comparable to the bow wave of a ship (which is also a shock-wave).[1] Just as a ship produces a bow wave throughout its entire journey, *so a supersonic aircraft generates a sonic bang throughout its entire flight at supersonic speed.* Many people still believe that the 'bang' occurs only once – at the instant of 'breaking the sound barrier'. The origin of this fallacy is the fact that any one person on the ground hears the bang only once – at the instant when he is enveloped by the shock-wave. (Similarly a child paddling at the edge of a river will be splashed only once by the bow-wave of a steamer, but the wave follows the boat until the end of the trip.)

What people on the ground in the path of the supersonic shock-wave actually experience is a bang. All sounds travelling through air are transmitted as pressure waves moving outwards from the disturbance which is the source of the sound. The passage of an SST causes a great disturbance, and the resulting pressure wave is a loud sound.

Overpressure

The severity of the sonic bang is usually expressed in terms of 'overpressure'. The increase in pressure ('overpressure') in an SST superonic shock-wave is of the order of 1.0 to 1.5

1. A ship produces a bow-wave and a stern-wave. So does an SST. With small supersonic aircraft the two shock-waves may merge into one, but with large transport aircraft the two waves are experienced as a double bang. See Fig. 4.

lb/sq. ft. Normally a person on the ground will be struck, simultaneously, by both the incident shock-wave from the aircraft and the reflected shock-wave from the ground. This 'pressure-doubling' effect is usually assumed when discussing sonic bangs, and on those terms the 'nominal' (or theoretical average) for the Concorde's sonic bang during supersonic cruise flight is about 2.0 sq. ft. The 'nominal' bang of the proposed US SST would be about 3.0 lb/sq. ft during cruise. During the acceleration-and-climb phase, the nominal overpressure is about 50 per cent greater: i.e. approximately 3.0 lb/sq. ft for Concorde and 4.0 lb/sq. ft for the US SST. Compared to normal atmospheric pressure at sea-level (about 15 lb/sq. *inch* or 2,160 lb/sq. *foot*) these pressure-increases are small, and this fact has given rise to many misconceptions, as will be explained.

The cause of the bang

As a subsonic aircraft flies along, the air moves aside smoothly, with negligible changes in pressures, and moves back in behind the aircraft again. There is no great compression, and no shock-wave is produced. With an SST the situation is very different: the air in front of an aircraft travelling at supersonic speed cannot get out of the way as it does in the case of a subsonic machine. Because the aircraft is travelling faster than the speed of sound in air (i.e. faster than air molecules normally travel) the air receives no advance 'push' as the plane approaches. It remains motionless. Not until the plane has approached within half an inch does the air begin to move out of the way – and it must then be forced aside within a few *millionths* of a second. The resulting motion of the air is vigorous. There is extreme local compression and heating, and a highly energetic shock-wave spreads out in a cone. The energy in the shock-wave from the plane as a whole is enormous; the power radiated outward in this wave amounts to 10,000 to 50,000 horsepower, comparable to the power requirement of an ocean liner such as the *Queen Elizabeth II*.

The shock-wave travels far, jolting everything it strikes. It continually spreads outward until the diameter is about 40 to 60 miles, beyond which the pressure rise is too small to be significant. (See Figure 4.) One of the two 'nesting' cones is

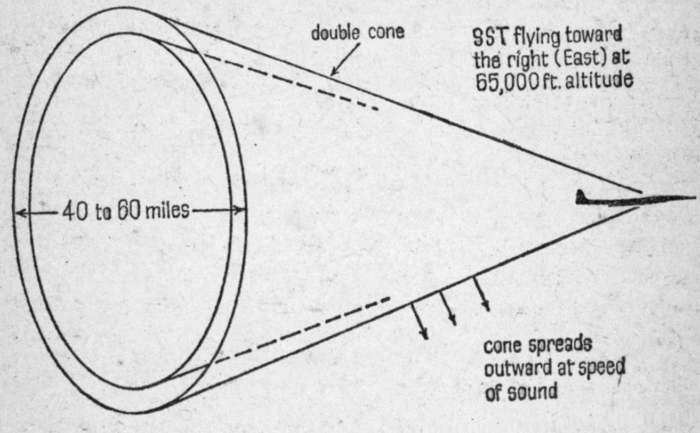

Fig. 4

derived from the nose of the plane, and the other from the tail. (See footnote on page 43.)

Bang-Zone

The bang-zone, or sonic bang carpet, is the portion of the earth's surface struck by the bang from an SST during supersonic flight. The bang-zone is as long as the supersonic flightpath itself: if an SST flew at supersonic speed for 2,000 miles, the length of the bang-zone would be 2,000 miles. The width of the bang-zone is about 50 miles if the SST is at cruising altitude of 60,000 to 70,000 ft. If the plane flies at lower altitude, the bang-zone is narrower – but the intensity is greater. The width depends also on wind and temperature variations in the atmosphere and may sometimes be as great as 80 miles.

Technicalities of the bang

'*Signatures*'. All the people, all buildings and other structures within the bang-zone are thus subjected to the effects of the supersonic shock-wave. This shock-wave comprises a very sudden rise in air pressure, followed by a rapid decrease to below normal pressure, and then by a further rapid rise back to normal. On a graph of pressure *vs.* time, the shock-wave is represented by an N-shaped curve, which is referred to as the 'signature'. Aircraft of different weights, lengths, and shapes produce different signatures.

Rise Time. The time interval in which the first pressure increase occurs, the *rise time*, is of great significance. When the rise time is very short, the bang is exceptionally startling.

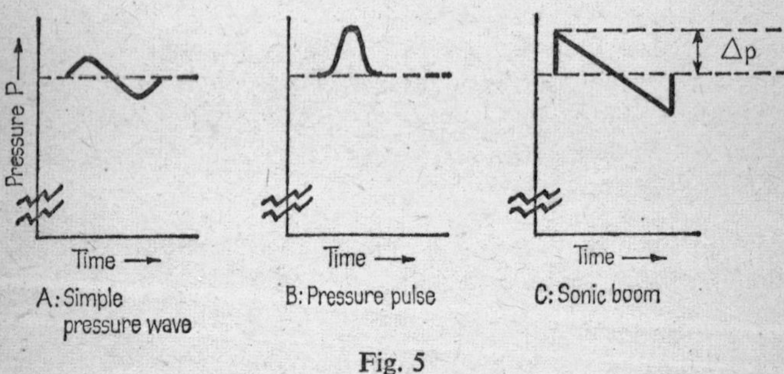

Fig. 5

Impulse and Intensity

Impulse is a term that takes into account not only the pressure rise but also the length of time during which the pressure acts. Crudely defined, it is the product of *pressure* and *time interval*; more exactly it is the integral of pressure excess with respect to time. The importance of impulse is easily understood; to produce damage, a bang must produce a large pressure and must *sustain* the pressure long enough for it to be effective. Both aspects (pressure and duration) are important. *Impulse* takes both aspects into account.

The SSTs are much longer than typical military supersonic planes and produce pressure pulses of longer duration. Thus SSTs' bangs tend to be more damaging for two reasons: greater overpressure (assuming a given flight altitude) and greater duration of the overpressure. In summary, the impulse is greater. For certain kinds of structures, impulse is the most important quantity and is a better measure of damage-potential than overpressure (ref. 58, 71).

The term *intensity* is often used informally to indicate the severity of a sonic bang. When used with greater accuracy, it means a quantity proportional to the square of the overpressure. Thus doubling the overpressure quadruples the intensity.

Superbangs

A superbang is a sonic bang that, at some given location, has an overpressure two or more times the nominal overpressure. (Detailed discussions of superbangs are presented in many reports by Lundberg. See *Aviation Week*, 27th March, 1967, or Baxter's impressive monograph, 'The SST: From Watts to Harlem in Two Hours' (ref. 8).)

There are four main causes of superbangs:

1. *Transition through Mach. 1.* When an aircraft is accelerating and reaches a speed very slightly exceeding the speed of sound in the atmosphere, the sonic bang produced is especially intense, and is a superbang. This effect occurs because impulses generated during the successive sectors of the flight arrive at the same place on the ground, simultaneously, and overlapping. Obviously, such superbangs are produced only locally. The ground area struck by such a superbang is small. The area has a curved, horseshoe shape; the overall width of the horseshoe is 10 to 25 miles and the length, measured parallel to the flightpath, is only 50 to 300 ft; the total area is about one square mile (ref. 60).

2. *Atmospheric Focusing.* If there are varying temperatures and wind velocities in the air through which the sonic-bang

shock-wave travels, focusing effects may occur. Consequently the overpressure at the ground is not uniform but varies considerably from one location to another. Some locations may experience little or no bang while others experience superbangs. A given house may receive twice the overpressure received by a neighbour's house a few hundred feet away. Typically, about one house in 500 in a given bang-zone will be hit by a double-overpressure bang and about one in 10,000 will be hit by a triple-overpressure bang, when an SST flies past at cruising altitude (ref. 60). Superbangs produced by atmospheric focusing are more frequent in summer than in winter (*Aviation Week*, 27th November, 1967).

3. *Reflection Effects*. If a sonic bang strikes smooth hard ground, or a city street, or a massive building, it is reflected. In the local region of reflection the bang overpressure may be twice the free-field overpressure. Ordinarily, bang overpressure is measured very close to the ground and accordingly the routine doubling that occurs here is already included in the measurement. Reflections from a deeply curved valley floor or from a cluster of massive buildings can sometimes triple the overpressure.

4. *Manoeuvre of the SST*. If the SST follows a curved path (up and down, or right and left), focusing effects occur and the bang travels with different intensities in different directions. Some houses may escape almost entirely; others may be struck by superbangs. Drastic changes in *speed* of the plane may also produce local superbangs.

Importance of superbangs

Though relatively rare, superbangs would be of great importance, for several reasons. First, the *absolute number* of buildings that would be struck by superbangs in a single day (if 200 SSTs were flying routinely over populated land at supersonic speed) would amount to about 2,000,000, and the number of man-superbangs per day would be about

10,000,000. Second, doubling the overpressure of a bang may result in damage *more* than twice that produced by a normal bang: a structure that remains unscathed by a 3 psf bang may be seriously damaged by a 6 psf bang. Third, because the superbangs are erratic, rather than predictable, engineers cannot plan ahead of time to make the bangs of 'marginally tolerable' intensity. Fourth, the existence of superbangs means that people must abandon any slight hope they may have had that they would 'get used to the bangs'. Even if a man somehow became accustomed to 2 psf bangs, he would be much startled and annoyed by a 4 or 8 psf bang.

It is expected that the Concorde SSTs would produce frequent superbangs with overpressure of 3 to 6 psf and the Boeing SSTs would produce frequent superbangs with 4 to 8 psf.

Seismic shock-wave. As the shock-wave in the atmosphere travels across the earth at supersonic speed, it induces in the ground an accompanying seismic shock-wave; this shakes buildings through their foundations, at the same instant that the aerial shock-wave strikes the upper parts. Very little is known about the effects of this seismic wave (76).

Resonance and related effects. As we have already noted, in comparison to the normal atmospheric pressure, the pressure involved in a supersonic shock wave is very small: it is an increase of the order of .05 of 0.1 per cent. This fact has been responsible for a great deal of confusion.

The attitude taken by the builders of the Concorde, and by the late Ministry of Technology, has been that such overpressures would not cause damage to 'normal and well-built structures' or to 'well-maintained buildings'.[2] Assurances have been given that the *overpressure* of Concorde's bangs would be no more than that of a 30 or 35 mph wind. In a recent letter, Mr T. P. Jones, of the Ministry of Technology's Concorde division, writes: 'The overpressure of Concorde's bang is equivalent to that caused by a wind of about 35 mph,

2. Statements from Min. Tech.

and the effect will in some circumstances (not of course in all) be comparable.'

Apparently a simple fact has been overlooked: the fact that the Concorde's sonic bang – unlike a 35 mph wind – is a bang (sometimes a tremendous bang); being a bang it can and does make objects vibrate; and if the objects are brittle (windows, mirrors, plaster, tiles, slates) and if the vibration is sufficiently severe, the objects break. This effect is not a matter of overpressure, but one of vibration induced by very loud bangs; in other words, of resonance and related effects (71).

The Anti-Concorde Project has spent much time and money in trying to make known the facts about resonance as a factor in sonic bang damage; the Concorde is now performing this task even more effectively – auditory and visual aids included. (Please see Chapter 6.)

What is an acceptable bang?

The question of an *acceptable bang* has been explored at length by the Swedish aeronautics expert B. K. O. Lundberg (refs. 56, 58, 60). After weighing the results from all major sonic bang tests made to date, and taking into account unavoidable variations in bang overpressure[3] and the widely varying vulnerability of people, he concludes that a bang having a nominal overpressure of about 0.1 pounds per square foot is about the most intense bang that could be accepted by the populations as a whole during the daytime and also at night. During the daytime only, 0.2 lb/sq. ft bangs might be acceptable – but it must be remembered that there are many people (night-shift workers, sick persons, infants) who sleep during the daytime.

The predicted overpressures of the SSTs are *ten to thirty*

3. One result of the current Concorde supersonic test flight programme has been confirmation of the fact that the intensity of the bang varies enormously even within a few hundred yards. People at one point may hear almost nothing, but a short distance away other people experience a tremendous bang, and material damage results. (Chap. 6.)

times the generally acceptable value of 0.1 lb/sq. ft adopted by Lundberg.

In the USA, Professor R. L. Bauer, Chairman of the Subcommittee on Human Response, Committee on SST-Sonic Boom, National Academy of Sciences, reviewed the available information and concluded that the acceptable limit was probably well below 0.75 psf (ref. 7). He gave consideration to adopting a value as low as 0.2 psf, but declined to designate any specific value. Proponents of the SST have been reticent as to what bang intensity is acceptable.

Is there a cure for the bang?

There is clear agreement among experts that there is no 'cure' for the sonic bang. The National Academy of Sciences' Committee on SST-Sonic Boom announced, after a two-year study led by Dr Raymond L. Bisplinghoff, Dean of Aeronautics at MIT, that '. . . future prospects for dramatic reduction in the intensities of sonic boom produced by supersonic aircraft are not readily apparent' (ref. 66). Dr A. J. Evans, NASA Director of Sonic Boom Research, stated that '. . . it's becoming obvious that the sonic boom will probably be unacceptable over land' (*Business Week*, 18th October, 1967). Various technical studies by NASA have also shown that there is no cure in sight for the sonic bang (ref. 106). Dr D. Hornig, White House Director of Science and Technology, told a House sub-committee on 28th February, 1968, that '. . . no major breakthrough can be expected in the foreseeable future' (*Aviation Daily*, 1st March, 1968).

In a 280-page Congressional staff report (ref. 47) it has been stated that 'The sonic boom is an inescapable by-product of forcing any large, heavy object through the air at speeds greater than the velocity of sound.'

Thus the consensus is that the sonic bang is to be regarded as a 'fact of nature'. Ocean-going ships create large bow waves. The sonic bang of an SST is in the same category.

The sonic bang depends partly on the lift required to keep the plane in the air, i.e. on the weight of the plane. It depends also on the detailed design of the plane – its configuration and streamlining. It is generally agreed that the sonic bang component due to the weight of the plane is unavoidable: it cannot be circumvented (unless the plane slows down to subsonic speed – or rises so high it is above the atmosphere. The component that depends on streamlining can be reduced by making the plane longer and more slender; but the existing designs are already so long and slender that stability, manoeuvrability, *and* passenger space are disappointing.

There have been various claims of partial 'cures', but these have turned out to be without real merit. Early in 1967 Northrup engineers proposed that an intense electrical discharge be maintained somehow just in front of the leading edge of the wing, and along the entire length of the wing, to heat the air there and start it moving out of the way before it is struck by the oncoming wing. But the idea seems impractical in many ways: *acres* of ionization would be required each second; an enormous power plant would be needed to generate the high-voltage electricity; an enormous electrode system would be needed; there would be danger from having electrical flashes so close to (possibly leaky) fuel tanks in the wings. Also there would be much added weight, and widespread interference with radio and TV signals received in the houses below. Dean R. L. Bisplinghoff, MIT aeronautics expert, has called the scheme '. . . untenable' (*Technology Review*, May 1968, p. 61). William T. Hamilton, a top Boeing executive, has declared the scheme to be 'impractical' (*Electronic News*, 29th January, 1968). Other Boeing engineers have declared the scheme would require 1,000 megawatts of electrical power, enough for a large city (*Aviation Weekly*, 3rd February, 1969).[4]

Likewise the suggestion by Dr Edwin L. Resler of Cornell's School of Aerospace Engineering proved to be of academic interest only. He proposed that the incipient shock-wave be somehow 'swallowed' by the aircraft engines

4. This idea received much favourable publicity when it was first advanced. The fact that it was soon pronounced to be impractical and untenable has received less notice.

and dissipated harmlessly. But no workable scheme for funnelling the shock-wave into the engines has been proposed, and the FAA has declared this system also to be of no practical significance (letter of 4th April, 1968, by C. L. Blake, Chief, Engineering Division, SST Development, FAA). *Aviation Daily* for 1st July, 1968, implies that Resler's idea could not be made practical for at least twenty years.

That it could *ever* be made practical seems unlikely – as is immediately apparent from consideration of the analogy with the bow and stern waves of a ship. Could a ship imaginably consume its own bow and stern waves? Moreover, the supersonic shock wave is in part related to the lift required to support the aircraft; could this component conceivably be consumed by the engines?

Palliatives exist, but are of limited effectiveness. Take the choice of altitude, for example. If the cruising altitude of an SST is increased, the bang overpressure at ground level decreases. However, the decrease is disappointingly small: it varies approximately as the first power (not the square!) of the altitude. More exactly, it varies approximately as

$$(\text{altitude})^{\frac{3}{4}}$$

as shown by Carlson and McLain in *International Science and Technology*, July 1966. In any event, the SSTs are already scheduled to fly at enormous altitude (55,000 to 70,000 ft, where the density of the air is only about 6 per cent that at sea-level); and even when at these altitudes, they would produce, at ground level, bang intensities of about 2.0 to 3.5 lb/sq. ft.

There is obviously an upper limit to the height at which SSTs can fly. Some have suggested that SSTs might fly *above* the atmosphere, where, in the absence of air, no supersonic shock-wave could be produced. But SSTs are aircraft – not rockets. They require the atmosphere to provide aerodynamic lift, and to provide oxygen for the engines and for the people on board.

As the fuel in an SST is gradually consumed (at the rate of ½ to 1 ton per minute, during the early part of the trip) the plane becomes lighter and the bang overpressure decreases somewhat, becoming about 10 to 20 per cent less at the end of the supersonic flightpath.

In mid-1969 Lockheed engineers proposed a 'theoretical' scheme for reducing the prevalence of sonic bangs. They pointed out that if an SST flies *barely* above the speed of sound (at Mach 1.15, say), if it flies at high altitude (above 40,000 ft), if the air is free of turbulence, and if the air near the ground is especially warm, the portion of the shock-wave travelling towards the ground will curve forward and may actually miss the earth. Typically, there *is* turbulence; thus the scheme would fail frequently. In any event, such a 'slow SST' would have little appeal to the airlines.

A light (smaller) SST would have a less intense bang than a large SST, other things being equal. But the economics of building and flying small SSTs, with small passenger capacity, become unfavourable, and the annoyance produced on the ground *per passenger carried* may actually increase.

CHAPTER SIX

The Effects of the Sonic Bang

Effects of sonic bangs – disturbance and damage

The important effects of sonic bangs at ground level, comprise *disturbance* to people and animals, and *damage* to buildings and structures. Professor Raymonde Bauer, of the Harvard School of Business Studies, wrote that '. . . the dominant consideration is how tolerable or intolerable human beings find sonic booms, not the dollar value of damaged plaster and window panes.'[1] It might be objected that if the material damage were great, and the disturbance slight, the opposite would apply; but in fact a supersonic shock which can damage buildings will be experienced by people as a very loud bang indeed. It will be very disturbing. And the further consideration arises that damaged windows, roofs, plaster, etc., are themselves a cause of disruption, annoyance, inconvenience and waste of time, far beyond the cash value of the repair. Damage to buildings is also a source of danger.

It has been suggested by SST proponents that disturbance by sonic bang is a 'subjective' matter. It has also been argued that SST sonic bangs would not damage 'well-maintained' buildings (with the corollary – implied or explicit – that if damage did occur the building could not have been 'well-maintained').

Years before any SST projects were commenced the fact was known that sonic bangs could create great disturbance and damage buildings. On 14th May, 1953, *The Times* published a letter, headed 'Supersonic flight: potential dangers

1. An address to the American Institute of Aeronautics and Astronautics, Philadelphia. 22nd October, 1968.

of the "bang" ', written by Mr A. H. Yates, Senior Lecturer in Aerodynamics, the College of Aeronautics, Cranfield:

> 'Sir: The Minister of Supply told the House of Commons on 11th May that "there was no solution in sight to the problem of the supersonic bang, and in fact we were probably in for some rather noisy times . . ." The prospect of unexpected and startlingly loud bangs from a hitherto silent sky is not a welcome one, and the Minister of Supply was right to warn us that no solution was in sight.'

After summarizing the physical cause of the sonic bang, and the effects to be expected from the passage of a supersonic machine at low altitude, Mr Yates concluded:

> 'It is clear that supersonic flying can be permitted only over the sea or at great heights, and disciplinary action against low flying will have to be much stricter than it is today. The danger of an enemy, or a thoughtless friend, raising the roof merely by flying past is a very real one.'

Military supersonic machines were flying in the mid-1950s, and on a number of occasions pilots accidentally flew too low or too fast, and as Mr Yates had predicted, disasters resulted. These incidents have little relevance to SST operation – during which the aircraft would fly at very high altitudes, and the shock-wave reaching the ground would be very much weaker than that concerned in these incidents. There does however remain the chance that an SST, in some emergency, might fly at supersonic speed at lower altitudes, and if this happened over a city, many millions of pounds worth of damage could result. This would of course be unintended; it would be an accident, and events of this type would not be expected in routine SST operation.

Let us now consider the effects of sonic bangs comparable to those which the SSTs would produce routinely. It was only during the latter part of 1970 that actual SST bangs, approaching the class of bang that would be produced by SSTs at normal operations height, full weight and full speed, have been produced. Previously, discussion of the likely or possible effects of SST sonic bangs had been based upon the observed effects of smaller military machines usually operating at altitudes lower than SST operating heights. Several series of tests, involving sonic bangs of this type, have been performed in the USA, and there is much evidence derived from effects of routine military supersonic flight in several countries.

This situation has given rise to much argument about the relevancy or otherwise of this evidence, which we shall discuss later in this chapter. Of the evidence available concerning damage caused by SST sonic bangs, the most important is that derived from the current series of supersonic flight tests with the Concorde prototype 002 on the Irish Sea route. Before discussing this it is desirable to consider such evidence as was previously available, and to decide whether adequate attention was given to it prior to the commitment of vast sums of government money to SST projects.

In September 1961, fourteen months before the Anglo-French Concorde Agreement was signed, Mr B. K. O. Lundberg, Director of the Swedish Institute for Aviation Research, gave a paper at the Cranfield Society Symposium, entitled 'Is Supersonic Aviation compatible with the sound development of civil aviation'. This paper was published by the Swedish Institute for Aviation Research in February 1962 (61). Mr Lundberg described in detail the problem of the sonic bang; he pointed out the inevitability of extensive prohibition of supersonic overflying; and he drew attention to many of the dangers (economic and otherwise) that would result from civil aviation 'becoming inextricably involved in a "supersonic race" '. Mr Lundberg's predictions have been proved well-founded. At Cranfield, he was talking to aerodynamicists. Did the warnings get through to a wider public – to the politicians? On 10th March, 1962 (still eight months before the Concorde agreement was signed), a further letter from Mr Yates was published in *The Times*. It was headed: 'PROGRESS WITH HAZARDS – EFFECT OF SONIC BOOMS', and it gave a clear statement of the effects to be expected from supersonic airliners, and it concluded: 'Many vested interests, from manufacturers to trade unions, are urging that supersonic airliners be built. Scientists can do no more than warn of the consequences. Politicians must read the evidence and decide.'

Whether they read the evidence or not, the politicians in the UK and France decided to enter the 'supersonic race'.

Sonic bang tests

No sonic bang tests were performed in the UK until 1967 – although by then very large sums of money had been committed to the Concorde. But in the USA, events took a somewhat more logical course: after it was realized that extra-severe bangs could cause serious damage to buildings, the US Government, hoping to proceed with its SST project, planned several series of sonic bang tests over cities.

Aviation officials expected to demonstrate that *typical* bangs do not damage buildings and do not annoy people appreciably. No SSTs existed. Therefore the tests were carried out with military supersonic planes. Being smaller and lighter than SSTs, the military planes normally produced bangs far milder than SSTs would produce. To compensate for this – partially, at least – the pilots flew their military planes at somewhat lower altitude. (As it turned out, the overpressures employed in the Oklahoma City tests were only about half those predicted for the Boeing SST.) Being shorter than SSTs, the military planes' bangs had a shorter duration and smaller impulse.

The US Government has published detailed reports on these tests, and it is a simple matter to compile statistics on the actual damage payments made (i.e. payments made up until the time the reports were written; many damage claims were then still in litigation). Additional information is now available from statements by the US Department of Justice and from Federal Court decisions.

St. Louis 1961–1962

There were 150 supersonic flights made over St Louis,

Missouri, in 1961 and 1962. The population of St Louis was then about 750,000. Thus the total number of man-bangs was (150) × (750,000) or about 113,000,000. (A man-bang is an individual act in which one bang strikes one person.) The official reports indicate that about 5,000 persons complained, 1,624 filed damage claims, and 825 of the claims were paid. The total payment was $58,684, corresponding to $519 per million man-bangs.

Oklahoma City, 1964

This is the most extensive sonic bang test ever made. For five months, sonic bangs were inflicted on Oklahoma City every hour on the hour (daytime only). Bang overpressure was monitored and the flights were arranged to produce gradually increasing overpressure from month to month; the average overpressure was about 1.3 lb/sq. ft (psf). The 1,254 flights over this city of 324,000 inhabitants produced 106,000,000 'man-bangs'; 15,452 persons complained and 4,901 persons filed damage claims (refs. 97, 99, 111). The largest payment was $10,000 to Mr Bailey Smith of 1803 NE 67 St, for serious damage done to his almost new $90,000 house (ref. 28, also personal communication from Mr Smith). Many of the largest claims were in litigation for many years. As a consequence of a 1968 verdict by the US Tenth District Court and a verdict of March 1969 by the US Tenth Circuit Court upholding that original verdict, a total of $94,015 damage payments was awarded in 1969 to supplement payments of $19,355 on claims settled in previous years. The aggregate payment was $123,370. This corresponds to $303 per million man-bangs (refs. 21, 22). (On 29th September, 1970, judgements on a further 53 cases were announced. Compensation totalling $95,277 was awarded; the largest award was for $4,200 and the smallest $550. Moves are now being made in Oklahoma City to have the time-limit during which the claims must be filed set aside, to enable 4,000 further claims to be brought before the courts.)

Oklahoma City residents found that sonic bangs broke window panes, cracked walls of plaster, tile, and bricks.

They found that the bangs shook shelves and caused dishes, tumblers, and vases to vibrate and eventually fall to the floor and break.

Chicago, 1965

The 49 flights over the city's 3,550,000 inhabitants resulted in 174,000,000 man-bangs, 7,128 complaints, 3,156 damage claims, and 1,464 payments aggregating $116,229, corresponding to $668 per million man-bangs (ref. 104, 3, p. 270).

Milwaukee, 1965

The 61 flights over 741,000 inhabitants resulted in 45,000,000 man-bangs, 953 complaints, 639 damage claims, and 259 claim payments aggregating $12,652, corresponding to $281 per million man-bangs (ref. 3).

Pittsburgh, 1965

The 50 flights over 604,000 inhabitants resulted in 30,000,000 man-bangs, 1,848 complaints, 1,102 damage claims, and 503 payments aggregating $30,808, corresponding to $1,027 per million man-bangs (ref. 3).

Edwards Air Force Base, California, 1966–1967

The 367 flights over 45,000 inhabitants resulted in 1,650,000 man-bangs, 62 complaints, 19 damage claims, and 16 claim payments aggregating $1,399, corresponding to $848 per million man-bangs (ref. 13). In these tests much attention was given to breakage of window panes both at the Air Force Base itself and in an adjacent village. The investigators went to the trouble of examining the Air Force Base window panes of principal interest *before and after* the bangs struck. They found the breakage rate to be 0.127 panes per million pane-bangs. The damage found in the nearby village (where verification was made with somewhat less care) was found to be 0.5 panes per million pane-bangs, i.e. four times as great (ref. 43).

Summary of US test results

The following table (p. 62) summarizes the results of the main sonic bang tests on buildings. It appears that the typical rate of damage payments was $400 to $700 per million man-bangs. A commonly used figure is $600 per million man-bangs (*Congressional Record*, 10th June, 1968, pp. H-4761–4762) (refs. 21, 22).

Other experience

US Air Force Experience

US Air Force planes' bangs do much damage each year in routine training flights and exercises. In the three-month period July–September 1967, $3,800,000 in sonic-bang damage claims were presented to the Air Force, according to a statement of 1st February, 1968 by Col. W. R. Arnold of the Office of the Judge Advocate General. In Illinois alone more than 1,000 complaints were made in that same period (*Chicago Tribune*, 16th September, 1967).

On 11th August, 1966, a bang from an Air Force plane struck the Canyon de Chelly National Monument in Arizona and loosened an estimated 80 tons of rock, which fell on ancient Indian cliff-dwellings and caused them irreparable damage. Additional damage was done by 83 sonic bangs in the subsequent four months (*National Parks Magazine*, March 1968; also *American Forests*, March 1967).

On 21st February, 1968, bangs produced in Mesa Verde National Park by jets from the Strategic Air Command caused 66,000 tons of rock to fall, according to estimates made by Meredith Guillet, Park Superintendent. He found that many of the '. . . several hundred Indian caves in the area have been cracked or damaged by the supersonic flights'. The rockslide temporarily closed one of the tourist roads (*Rocky Mt News*, 25th April, 1968; also letter of 25th April, 1969, by K. L. Lundquist, Archaeologist, National Park Service, Mesa Verde National Park).

Analysis of Damage Payments from US Sonic Bang Tests

City	*Population*	*Total number of man-bangs*	*Complaints*	*Claims filed*	*Claims paid*	*Amount paid*	*Amount paid per million man-bangs*
Oklahoma City (1964)	324,253	406,000,000	15,452	4,901	289	$218,338	$ 538
Chicago (1965)	3,550,404	174,000,000	7,128	3,156	1,464	116,229	668
St. Louis (1961–62)	750,026	113,000,000	5,000	1,624	825	58,648	519
St. Louis (1965)	750,026	17,000,000	1,390	491	215	17,036	1002
Milwaukee (1965)	741,324	45,000,000	953	639	259	12,652	281
Pittsburgh (1965)	604,332	30,000,000	1,848	1,102	503	30,808	1027
Edwards AFB (1966–67)	45,000	1,650,000	62	19	16	1,399	848

Experience in Europe

In France, it has been considered essential for military aircrews to carry out supersonic training and exercises over the territory which they might be required to defend. There has therefore been considerable experience of the sonic bang in France. The *Guardian* (London) reported (5th August, 1967):

> 'The French Government paid out about £143,000 last year in compensation for damage caused to private property by supersonic booms.
>
> A spokesman for the Armed Forces Ministry said today the compensation was paid following 2,870 complaints about the effects of supersonic bangs in spite of new flying regulations governing military aircraft – the only planes allowed to over-fly French territory at supersonic speeds. But many Frenchmen fear that the situation will be aggravated by the introduction of the Concorde.
>
> ***Three Killed***
>
> A fresh wave of anxiety swept France this week when a farmhouse in the North-west collapsed, killing three people. Survivors said that they heard a loud sonic boom just before the roof beams fell in.
>
> The Ministry spokesman said that two years ago military pilots were prohibited from breaking the sound barrier over populated areas or at a height of under 30,000 feet – *Reuter*.'

Comparatively little information is generally available about the total amount of damage that has resulted from supersonic military flying over France, or the amounts that have been paid in compensation by the Government. But an immensely valuable report, 'Effects of Supersonic Flight', by Michael Parent – principal inspector of historic monuments in France – was published in the January–March issue of *Les Monuments Historiques de la France* (ref. 76).

In the UK. As already remarked, there were no sonic bang tests before 1967; and military pilots have for many years been instructed not to fly overland at supersonic speeds. In some areas near the sea, as, for instance, in Western Wales, in Devon and Cornwall, and in Norfolk, sonic bangs have been experienced. Claims for damage have been made, and have been paid. Development of the Concorde, in the early years, and indeed up to 1967, had proceeded on the assumption that the Concorde's sonic bang would be 'acceptable', and that people would get used to the bang. In July 1967 the Ministry of Technology staged a brief series of supersonic tests. During one week, eleven flights were made, four over London, five at Bristol, and two over Dorset. The tests were made with Lightning fighter aircraft. The Lightnings' bangs were far less intense than the Concorde's bangs were expected to be. Announcing the tests, Mr Stonehouse (Minister of State at the Ministry of Technology) insisted that the Lightnings' bangs would be 'at intensities known from previous experience to be well below those likely to cause damage'. On 18th July, in the House of Commons, Mr Anthony Wedgwood Benn (Minister of Technology) referred to the bangs as 'mild' and he said that they were 'at an intensity well below that of supersonic airliners'. Mr Ivor Richard, MP, received no satisfactory answer to his question: How much worse will the airliners be than the test flights? No official arrangements were made to investigate public reaction to the bangs, but the *Guardian* commissioned a public opinion survey at Bristol, on the basis of which it reported on 20th July, 1967, that:

> 'Nearly two-thirds of the population of Bristol were frightened, startled, or annoyed by the sonic booms to which they were subjected last week. The rest either did not mind or were resigned to them.
>
> This is the central result of an opinion survey carried out for the *Guardian* at the end of the Government's test programme there. And Londoners who are now hearing the booms for themselves may like to know that according to the survey, 53 per cent of Bristolians who heard the

booms think they are likely to cause serious discomfort to people, and 42 per cent believe this will be true for animals . . .'

Nineteen months later on 17th December, 1968, Mr Benn announced in the House of Commons that more than £4,000 had been paid to people claiming personal injury or damage to property caused by the 1967 tests. 788 claims were made and, according to *The Times* of 10th December, 1968:

'Payments were made in respect of 515 of the claims, 270 were rejected and three were still under discussion.

Three of the settled claims involved personal injury and a total of £199 7s. 6d. was paid.

The largest number of paid claims, 246, was for damage to glass; £1,101 1s. 1d. was paid out. But the biggest total figure, £1,395 5s. 2d., was paid for damage to ceilings. Here, settled claims numbered 93.

TABLE OF CLAIMS

	Number of claims	*Number of payments*	*Total amount of payments* £	s.	d.
Personal injury	8	3	199	7	6
Injury or damage to animals (including eggs)	4	3	49	7	6
Damage to:					
glass	338	246	1,101	1	1
ceilings	126	93	1,395	5	2
roofs and chimneys	84	58	525	11	5
gutterings	19	14	162	6	0
walls	51	21	101	0	0
ornaments	19	15	77	8	0
vehicles	13	5	37	11	6
Miscellaneous	123	57	470	10	8
Under discussion	3	—	—		
TOTAL	788	515	4,119	8	10

395 claims were met in the London area, 116 in the Bristol Channel area and 4 in Dorset.

Mr Benn, who was answering a request by Mr Ben Whitaker, Labour MP for Hampstead, for a statement on the bang tests, said:

"My department received some 12,000 complaints (some 3,400 by telephone) from people in the areas affected at the times the bangs were made. Some 9,600 complaints were from the London area and some 2,300 from the Bristol Channel area.

"Many of the complaints were in general terms, expressing disapproval, fear or anxiety."

Mr Benn said that the tests were "confined to the strictly limited purpose of providing wider experience for the public of the nature of sonic bangs. It was not intended to provide a statistical analysis from which conclusions could be drawn of public reaction to supersonic flying overland."

He added: "The information obtained from these tests will be useful to my department in the continuing programme of research it is conducting in collaboration with the American and French authorities into the nature and effects of sonic bangs.

"No decision has been taken, or could have been taken at this stage, on what restrictions, if any, should be imposed on supersonic flight overland." '

This last sentence expressed the official view, given in Parliamentary replies on many occasions that 'no decision has yet been taken on what restrictions should be imposed on supersonic flight overland'. And yet, only 17 months later, in May 1970, no further sonic bang tests having been made, the Government in which Mr Benn was still Minister of Technology published its White Paper on the *Protection of the Environment* (Cmnd. 4373) which stated:

'Apprehension has been expressed about the nuisance and damage which might be caused by sonic bangs when supersonic civil airliners, the first of which in the western world will be the Anglo-French Concorde, come into service. The Government have taken powers in the Civil Aviation Act 1968 to regulate or prohibit flights of aircraft over the United Kingdom at supersonic speeds. True, Britain is a small country, and supersonic speeds are not attained within about the first hundred miles after take-off, nor maintained for about the last hundred miles before landing. *Nevertheless, it is the Government's view that commercial supersonic flights which could cause a boom to be heard on the ground should be banned and they intend to publish draft proposals to this effect with a view to consultation with all those concerned.*'

Then, a few weeks later came the General Election, and a change of government. Among the opponents of the Concorde it was thought that much effort would be needed to bring the new Conservative Government up to the position, on supersonic overflying, that the Labour Government had so recently adopted.

But in September, after only two supersonic flights by the British Concorde over parts of the Irish Sea route, Mr Eldon Griffiths, MP, Joint Parliamentary Secretary, Ministry of Housing and Local Government, announced that his government intended to publish 'proposals for the banning of commercial flying at supersonic speed over the United Kingdom'.

Effects of Concorde's sonic bangs.

During the autumn of 1970 the supersonic flight testing of the Concorde on the Irish Sea route has provided people in western Scotland, Northern Ireland, south-west Wales and Cornwall with a considerable amount of experience of the Concorde's own sonic bangs. The first flight on September 1 was awaited with great interest and some apprehension. Most of the observers were at St David's, Pembrokeshire, but in the event the Concorde flew many miles off-course and the bang at St David's was slight. Along the track beneath the flight-path of the aircraft, however, the bang was very severe. There were many reports of damage including cracked and broken windows, slates falling from roofs, broken mirrors. There were reports of stampeding cattle and ponies, hysterical hens and turkeys, and panicking flocks of sheep. 'Children screamed and ran crying into their homes'; a farmer and his wife, baling hay 'both felt that they had been physically hit' (*Western Telegraph*, 10th September, 1970). Subsequent flights have resulted in a great number of similar reports; they have also confirmed that the bang varies greatly over small distances on the ground, and that it 'can be shattering' (*South Wales Echo*, 5th October). Members of Parliament, County Councils and other local authorities, branches of the National Farmers' Union, and many other groups have protested vehemently about the bangs, and have called for the cancellation of the tests or the changing of the route.

The Ministry of Aviation Supply has received several hundred complaints and several hundred claims for compensation for damage – possibly the largest being the claim of a Cornish smallholder for £705 in respect of damage to his house and 'the shock, worry and disturbance suffered by himself and his wife' (*Daily Telegraph*, 2nd December). This claim is being supported by Mr John Nott, MP, who described the damage to property caused by Concorde as 'an outrage' (the *Guardian*, 2nd December, 1970).

Here are some characteristic headlines from newspaper reports on the tests:

Concorde boom upsets farmers (*The Times*, Sept. 3). Concorde boom blamed for damage (*Daily Telegraph*, Sept. 3). Concorde flight brings flood of complaints (*Western Mail*, Sept. 3). MP may demand Concorde ban (*Western Mail*, Sept. 3). Concorde brings terror down on the farm (*The Sun* – northern edition, Sept. 3). Concorde panicked animals, say angry farmers (*Liverpool Daily Post*, Sept. 3). Concorde frightens islanders (*Sunday Telegraph*, Sept. 6). Keep the Concorde away says Bishop of St David's (*South Wales Post*, Sept. 24). No more Concorde tests, demand Council (*Western Mail*, Sept. 28). 1,210 mph Concorde superboom starts a storm (*Evening News*, Oct. 2). Concorde booms to new row (*Daily Mail*, Oct 3). NFU asks for 002 test ban (the *Guardian*, Oct. 5). MPs and farmers protest after 'deafening' boom – Storm over off-course Concorde

(*Liverpool Daily Post*, Oct. 3).1,200 mph Concorde shakes Ulster (*Daily Telegraph*, Oct. 3). Concorde booms bring call for a ban (*Western Mail*, Oct. 3). Buildings shake, windows crack in double boom – Anger as Concorde hits 1,200 mph (*Western Mail*, Oct. 3). Concorde draws loud protests (*The Times*, Oct 3). Concorde: 'It's sheer lunacy' (*West Briton*, Oct. 15). NFU may sue Ministry over Concorde row (*Western Telegraph*, Oct. 15). Concorde disaster fund for nurserymen (*Gardeners Chronicle*, Oct 16). Loudest – and fastest – Concorde jolts city (*West Briton*, Oct 29). Concorde at Mach. 2 is loudest yet (*Western Evening Herald*, Nov. 13). Biggest jolt yet from Concorde (*West Briton*, Nov. 19). End this Concorde folly, say MPs (*Western Mail*, Nov. 19).

Annoyance caused by sonic bangs

Kinds of annoyance

As has already been indicated, sonic bangs cause annoyance because they break such things as windows and mirrors, bring down plaster from walls and ceilings, and make slates and tiles slip from roofs. They also cause annoyance in that they are experienced as a sudden and unexpected noise. People dislike very loud bangs, and for good reason; technically, the reaction to a bang is known as *startle effect*.

The suggestion that we can 'get used to the bangs' ignores the fact that if we somehow *could* train ourselves out of the 'startle' response, this would be detrimental to our welfare. In the modern world alert responses are certainly no less essential than at all other periods in history and prehistory.

Degree of annoyance

No adequate definition of degree of annoyance from sonic bangs exists. Most acoustics experts, noticing that the bangs are loud, have concentrated their efforts on measuring the *loudness* of the bang; they have compared this loudness with the loudness of noises that are more familiar to us – such as aircraft take-off noise. To date, no one has developed a businesslike method of measuring annoyance due to the startle effect itself.

In the Oklahoma City sonic bang tests, much effort was given to questioning the inhabitants and finding how annoying they considered the bangs. Results of the questionnaires show that a majority of the inhabitants found the bangs annoying, and, after several months of being subjected to bangs every hour during the daytime, 27 per cent of the persons interrogated declared that they could never learn to live with them (ref. 99). It is noteworthy that those bangs had an average overpressure of about 1.3 lb/sq. ft, i.e. only about half the overpressure that those of the Boeing SSTs would have. Also, the bangs occurred only during the daytime. They occurred on a fixed schedule and as a consequence some of the surprise element was absent.

In the Edwards Air Force Base tests, reported in detail in the official report (q.v.), great effort was made to evaluate annoyance of the bangs. Of the 300 persons serving as 'test subjects', some were newcomers to sonic bangs and others had been familiar with them for a year or more. The 300 persons were repeatedly struck by sonic bangs from military B-58 supersonic planes, and their opinions were then polled. It was found that 40 per cent of the newcomers and 27 per cent of the habituated persons '. . . rated the B-58 booms of nominal peak overpressure 1.69 lb/sq. ft as being less than *just acceptable* to *unacceptable*'.

The annoyance would have been much greater if the tests had not been biased in several ways. The people subjected to the bangs were warned one or two minutes before each bang, with the result that most of the surprise was eliminated. (If you are sincerely trying to see how startling a sudden loud noise is to a person, you do not tell him just ahead of time, 'Get ready! I'm now going to startle you!') The people were adults. They were in good health. They participated in the tests voluntarily. They were relaxed and at leisure when the bangs struck, and the overpressure (1.69 lb/sq. ft was much less than the overpressure that the Boeing SSTs would produce (2.0 to 3.5 lb/sq. ft).

The fact that the people objected so strongly to these bangs despite these 'softening' circumstances is impressive.

Polls taken after the tests in St Louis and Chicago showed that about 40 per cent of the people were greatly annoyed by the bangs. In a poll taken in France, 35 per cent of the persons questioned said they '... definitely could not tolerate' ten a day (ref. 14).

Damage estimates

It has already been noted that the British Government has taken powers to ban all SST overflying in the UK, although at the time of writing no such restriction is operative. It is extremely likely that other countries will similarly ban supersonic overflying.

Scientists of the Citizens' League against the Sonic Boom have calculated that the cost of damage that would be caused by fleets of SSTs operating over the USA would be of the order of £1m per day. (*Correlation of public reaction to sonic-boom-induced property damage*. CLASB.)[2] It is important to note that similar large damage costs could be expected in much smaller areas that are densely populated. Thus a single supersonic flight over England and Wales (with a population density 17 times that of the USA) might impose its sonic bang upon as many people as a flight across the USA. This estimate includes the cost of immediate damage, but makes no allowance for inevitable cumulative effects. Michel Parent (Principle Inspector of Historic Monuments, France) has written (76):

> 'How many buildings are being secretly damaged little by little? ... How much invisible, but nevertheless *real* damage is being done? And will it result, in the future, after repeated bangs, in irreversible deterioration? The gradual attrition of the mortar between the stones, the gradual shaking-down of the infilling of rubble-filled walls, the falling of particles down into cracks, which

2. Ref. 22.

slowly but inexorably are forcibly widened, are some of the less spectacular aspects of the effects of sonic bangs, which are worrying cathedral architects just as much as the possibility of more spectacular damage.'

Could the SSTs detour around population centres, so as to minimize the number of houses banged? To a very slight extent only. The only merit of the SST is in shortening flight time, and every detour lengthens the route, increases the flight time, and increases the fuel cost. In any event, the manoeuvrability of the SST is poor. The difficulty and expense of turning a corner were emphasized in a speech of 15th November, 1967, by General J. C. Maxwell, then FAA Head of SST Development, at the National Air Safety Meeting: 'At supersonic speed we aren't going to be able to afford much turning – it will just use up too much fuel.' For an SST to make a sharp turn would take up to 100 miles, so only very slight turns would be feasible. As the SST's bang-zone is 50 miles wide, there would seldom be any chance of avoiding all cities and towns.

Dr Shurcliff (84, p. 52) calculated that world operation of fleets of SSTs, without restriction on supersonic overflying, might result in half a million damage claims per day. Possibly the number of jobs 'created' by the building of the SSTs would be far surpassed by the number of jobs 'created' in processing the claims and in repairing the damage.

Damage payment dilemma

Some have argued that the sonic bang problem is largely solved if one can arrange to make *prompt* damage payments to the owners of the houses damaged by the bangs.

But to arrange fair and prompt damage payments would be virtually impossible, since:

> 'The homeowner will often be unable to prove that his glass, plaster, masonry, etc., was indeed damaged by the bang, and not by ground settlement or other cause.
>
> The homeowner will not be able to find out which air-

craft which pilot, which airline, or which nationality of airline was responsible for damage caused at a specified time. The plane is 20 to 40 miles away by the time the bang strikes the house, and is then out of sight.

Damage can be cumulative – a result of bangs from many planes over a period of many weeks. Blame for such damage cannot be ascribed to any *one* plane.

The expense of filling a claim for small damage may exceed the amount claimed for the damage.

An agency engaged in evaluating the paying claims may find itself enmeshed in prolonged and bitter disputes with tens of thousands of homeowners every month. Thousands of claims adjusters may be needed, and hundreds of lawyers. Agency and homeowner alike will be relying on circumstantial evidence. Injustice will be frequent, and hard-feeling likewise.'

The indisputable facts are, that in the UK it took the Ministry of Technology nearly eighteen months to process some 788 claims which arose from the *eleven* short flights in 1967; in France it took three years to settle the question of compensation arising from the deaths of three people who were killed in August 1967 when a sonic bang knocked down a farmhouse; and in the USA it has taken six years to settle the claims which arose from the 1964 tests at Oklahoma City. In view of these vast lengths of time which bureaucracy has required to process such comparatively small numbers of claims, whatever would be the situation in an era of commercial supersonic overland flight? It has been calculated, for example, that in the USA the processing of claims would require a department equal in size to the present Internal Revenue Service.[3] In this context, the concept of SST as an agency for *saving time* loses meaning.

To make damage payments for human annoyance and human suffering from the bang would be extremely difficult. How can one put a price on a sleepless night? An aggravated headache or ulcer? An irritable mood? A permanent

3. Correlation of Public Reaction to sonic-boom-induced property damage. (Ref. 22.)

feeling of despair at forever surrendering peace and quiet in the home? One may ask also about a heart patient under doctor's orders to avoid becoming excited or startled, or a house painter who is startled and falls from a ladder, or a nervous and pregnant woman who miscarries as a result of startle effect. An eminent eye-surgeon has aready warned that eye-surgeons must not be startled during a delicate eye operation; an involuntary motion of the surgeon's hand might produce permanent blindness (letter of 12th September, 1968, by Dr Henry F. Allen, Director of Post-Graduate Programme in Ophthalmology, Harvard Medical School).

How would a museum director collect damages for priceless objets d'art, or archaeological specimens, damaged by broken glass from a museum skylight? How could a symphony orchestra director collect for the harm done to a tape recording of a symphony interrupted by sonic bang?[4] How can a vacation-resort hotel-owner collect for loss of customers who dislike holidaying in a region lying beneath a main SST flight route?

In the UK, when the arrangements for paying compensation for damage caused by Concorde during its test flights were announced, it was made clear that no compensation would be paid for annoyance.

Will supersonic flight overland be banned?

The supersonic projects were commenced upon the assumption that supersonic flight overland would be accepted. It assumed that 'people will get used to the booms'. As recently as the autumn of 1969, BAC referred to 'the assumption that supersonic flight will be allowed only over the oceans or over

4. 'The boom penetrated the recording studios in the Kingsway Hall, where Miss Joan Sutherland was recording highlights from her repertoire with the Covent Garden Orchestra. "Donizetti's Daughter of the Regiment" bore the registration of the sonic boom. The Decca Record Company, which was making the record, last night was considering seeking compensation from the Ministry for the cost of keeping artist and orchestra for a further recording session.' – The *Guardian*, 20th July, 1967.

areas with sparse populations' as an 'extremely pessimistic assumption'. 'Concorde's makers do not expect that its sonic boom will be unacceptable to the great majority of the public' (16, p. 20).

This clearly implies that the boom might be unacceptable to a minority, which, by definition, would be composed of the most vulnerable people: children, old people, people who are ill or worried, hospital patients, people whose occupations require quiet conditions. It is implied that these people – and the inhabitants of 'areas with sparse populations' can be boomed regardless. These same assumptions have been made by the supporters of the US SST.

The importance of noise, sleep disturbance, startle, stress, as factors in the causation of physical, psychiatric, and psychosomatic illness are well known, and it now seems certain that supersonic overflying will be extensively prohibited. The attitudes of several countries to this question are discussed in Appendix 4. The UK Government has not yet come to a decision. In May 1970, in its White Paper on the environment, the Labour Government stated its view that 'commercial supersonic flights which could cause a boom to be heard on the ground could be banned'. On 14th September, a Conservative minister, Mr Eldon Griffiths, MP, stated: 'The Government will shortly be publishing proposals for the banning of commercial flying at supersonic speeds over the United Kingdom . . . I can assure you we will carefully consider the views of all concerned on these proposals before arriving at a final decision. There will be the widest possible discussion with the airlines and all interested parties.' In the USA, the Senate voted on 2nd December, 1970, to prohibit commercial supersonic overflights.

Please see also Appendix Four: *'Other countries' attitudes towards the sonic bang'*.

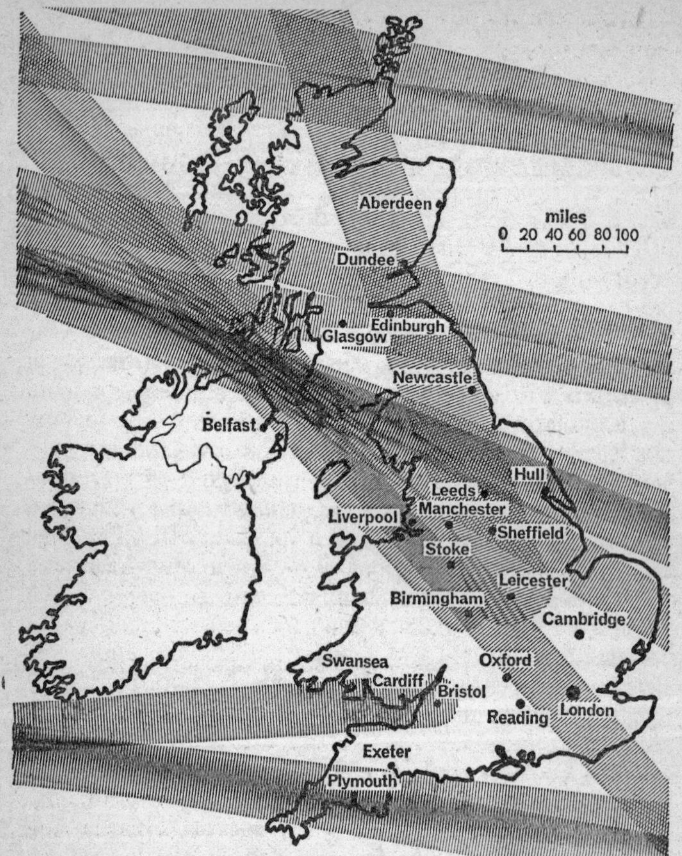

Fig. 6: *Map showing possible supersonic routes over the UK.*

Bang-paths forty miles wide are shown (the actual width might be greater). Routes have been adjusted to take into account the ban on supersonic flights over the Republic of Ireland. The map illustrates the obvious fact that as more countries ban supersonic overflights, the flight lanes will become increasingly concentrated over territories from which they are not banned. This will inevitably lead to demands from those territories for prohibition.

The extra-wide bang-path, NNW from London, represents a transpolar route such as might be taken by a large, long-range SST, if such a machine were developed.

CHAPTER SEVEN

Degradation of the Environment

Preceding chapters have dealt with the phenomenon of the sonic bang and with its effects. However, as yet, little has been said of the various other aspects of supersonic transport which mitigate against the environment.

The huge quantities of water vapour which a fleet of supersonic aircraft would release into the atmosphere could cause massive clouds, and could raise the humidity, thereby altering the radiation balance. Take-off and landing noise, pollution (both by partly-burnt kerosene and by poisonous fuel additives), a predicted world fuel shortage arising from the vast kerosene consumption of SSTs, the effects of sonic bangs on animals, the spoiling of the peace of remote parts of the countryside, the problems attendant on overflying the North Atlantic: all these factors must also be taken into consideration.

Contamination of Upper Atmosphere

Dr V. J. Schaefer, world-famous atmospheric physicist and Director of Atmospheric Sciences Research Center at Albany, New York, has pointed out that SSTs, discharging in the order of 150,000 tons of water vapour *daily* (from fuel combustion) into the upper atmosphere might produce 'global gloom' (*This Week*, 11th August, 1968, p. 4). The water vapour would linger, suspended, in the form of clouds.

The widespread use of supersonic transports will introduce large quantities of water vapour into the stratosphere. The weight of water vapour released is about 40 per cent greater than the weight of the fuel consumed. Four hundred SSTs flying four trips per day might release an amount of water vapour per day that is 0.025 per cent of that naturally present in the altitude range in which the flights occur. The introduction of this additional water vapour into the stratosphere can produce two effects which may be important:

(1) Persistent contrails might form to such an extent that there would be a significant increase in cirrus clouds;

(2) There could be a significant increase in the relative humidity of the stratosphere even if there were no significant increase in the extent of cirrus cloudiness.

Both effects would alter the radiation balance and thereby possibly affect the general circulation of atmospheric components. Of greater significance may be the local contamination one can expect from a high concentration of flights over the North Atlantic. If half the activity is concentrated over 5 per cent of the earth's surface, local contamination would be ten times larger than calculated above on a global basis or about 0.25 per cent per day of the naturally present water vapour. However, the local concentration of water vapour from flights on crowded routes may spread out rapidly and be of no real significance.

Although it would appear that geophysical effects are probably minor, they certainly should not be neglected. Data required include information relevant to the horizontal mixing times within the stratosphere and to the resident time of gases within the stratosphere. With these parameters at hand, it should be possible to construct a numerical model of the stratosphere to determine more accurately the possible radiative effects on the general circulation.

The SST Review Committee and the Proxmire Committee both considered this a problem (please see Appendices Two and Three, pages 122 and 146.

Airport noise

SSTs require very powerful engines, which are inherently very much noisier than those of current commercial aircraft. This problem is considered in the reports of both President Nixon's SST Review Committee and the Proxmire Committee (please see Appendices Two and Three–pages 122 and 146). The SST Review Committee, for example, points out that the Boeing SST's engines 'are fundamentally noisier than the fan engines that are optimum for the subsonic jets'. A Swiss airline official has said: 'I am deeply worried about the SST's sideline noise during take-off . . . populated areas *abreast of the runway* will be flooded with noise that exceeds today's noise level, generated by DC-8s and 707s, by a very, very wide margin' (A. Baltensweiler, Swissair, in *Air Travel Official Airline Guide* of February 1968, p. 14). R. L. Bisplinghoff, former Dean of Aeronautics at Massachusetts Institute of Technology, has stated: '. . . where the SST is noisier than other airplanes is in its sideline noise . . . here we are definitely over anything that is now flying and we have no immediate prospect of reducing this to the level of the current subsonic jets' (*Congressional Hearings*, 9th October, 1959) (ref. 94 p. 28). *Guardian* (7th October, 1968), the Concorde may be 'more than twice as noisy as today's aircraft in terms of lateral noise and, to make matters worse, the lower frequencies of its engines will penetrate indoors more easily'.

The engine roar at landing, too, will be great. The Concorde, for example, is designed to land at 180 mph with an upward tilt of 10.8 degrees and *with engines on full*. According to *Aerospace Technology* (of 20th May, 1968, p. 53), the Concorde 'may show a rather startling 124 PNdB figure during approach, primarily because its engine inlets cannot be choked'. (The symbol *PNdB* stands for *perceived noise, in decibels*. The decibel is a logarithmic unit. By way of illustration: 50 PNdB corresponds to the amount of noise in a typical quiet living room, 90 PNdB corresponds to the noise beside a motorway on which trucks are going by at high speed, and 120 PNdB is almost unbearably loud.)

What loudness is acceptable? In January of 1969 the FAA circulated a proposed regulation (Docket 9337, Notice 69-1) suggesting an ideal goal (ceiling on noise at airport) of 80 EPNdB and proposing to limit noise of the very heavy (600,000 lb) subsonic planes to about 108 EPNdB. (The distinction between PNdB and EPNdB is slight, and too technical to explain here.) Specific regulations were being prepared for release prior to the end of 1970.

Strong doubts were expressed in March 1969 by President Nixon's *SST ad hoc Review Committee* (see Appendix 2) as to whether the Boeing SST could conform to reasonable standards of noise. The Committee indicated that the noise might well be excessive and could cause various adverse effects, including some or all of these: hearing loss, cardiovascular and neurologic changes, and glandular and respiratory troubles. It concluded that '... significant numbers of people will file complaints and resort to legal action, and ... a very high percentage of the exposed population will find the noise intolerable.'

That the regulatory agencies can permit such engine roar at airports is hard to believe, inasmuch as the trend of recent Congressional action has been to *reduce* airport noise. On 24th July, 1968, President Johnson signed bill HR-3400 authorizing and requesting the FAA to set satisfactory limits on such noise. Many Congressmen cited the agony of suburbanites living near airports and pleaded for establishment of lower limits on noise. Court actions, too, have recently favoured outright reduction in airport noise – or making substantial damage payments to the persons affected. Total damage claims, because of intolerable aircraft take-off and landing noise, by persons living close to Los Angeles International Airport now exceed $*5 billion*, according to *Aviation Daily* of 31st January, 1969.

However, it is very important to note that when in 1970 the UK Government produced proposals for the regulation of aircraft noise, the Concorde was specifically excused from having to comply.[1]

Concorde at Heathrow

On September 13th, 1970, as a result of bad weather at its home base, Concorde prototype 002 was diverted to Heathrow airport, London. *The Times* reported, the following day, that there had been 'a wave of complaints from people living

1. A statement by M. Henri Ziegler, head of the French side of the Concorde project, expressing doubts about the practicality of fitting 'silencers' to Concorde, is quoted on p. 81.

under its approach path. . . . Heathrow airport's telephone exchange was inundated with callers ringing to complain'. 'Slates were rattled loose from roofs and sent hurtling to the ground and crockery shaken from shelves as Concorde passed overhead . . .' (*Balham and Tooting News*, 18th Sept.) A resident of Richmond, Surrey, said: 'Concorde made more noise than a dozen VC-10s going overhead. People's lives will be hell if Concorde sounds like that every time she lands or takes off' (*Daily Record*, 14th Sept., 1970).

Commenting upon suggestions that the engine-noise of production-model Concordes would be reduced, M. Henri Ziegler, head of SNIAS (the French manufacturers of Concorde) has referred to the difficulty of imposing upon the manufacturers and operators, silencers which result in reduced power and increased weight; this will not happen unless some penalty on aircraft noise – for example a noise tax – is imposed (*Le Monde*, 24th September, 1970).

On 2nd December, 1970, the US Senate voted to impose upon SSTs the same limit for airport sidelines noise as that set for subsonic aircraft, i.e. 108 EPNdB. It is extremely unlikely that either the US SST or the Concorde could conform to this standard.

World Fuel Consumption

An article in the *Observer* of 30th August, 1970, predicted a world oil shortage within fifteen years, if British and American aircraft manufacturers were to sell their planned total of supersonic airliners (300 Concordes and 80 Boeing SSTs). Even by 1980, a fleet this size would demand that 320 million metric tons of crude oil be produced each year. This is near one-third of the total planned oil consumption of Western Europe or the US in the same year – some 8 per cent of expected total *world* oil consumption.

American officials have spoken of an ultimate market for 1,200 SSTs (this includes Boeings, Concordes, and Tu–144s). BAC say that one Concorde will consume 18,600 gallons on a 3½-hour London–New York flight. To justify their investment in these aircraft, airlines will have to operate four transatlantic flights by each plane each day: 14 hours flying in every 24. At this rate, over one year a Concorde would consume 100,000 metric tons of kerosene.

If, as planned, there are 300 Concordes in service by 1980, these planes will burn 30 million tons of kerosene in that year. With the addition of 80 Boeings in that year (burning 16 million tons of kerosene each year), the total annual kerosene consumption by the entire supersonic fleet in 1980 will reach 46 million tons.

'But to produce one ton of kerosene means refining at least seven tons of crude oil. The 1980 supersonic fleet will take up 322 million tons of unrefined petroleum.

'To appreciate what this means, one must look at the official projected 1980 figures for crude oil demand, published in the International Petroleum Encyclopedia: North America, 1,120 million tons; Western Europe, 1,100 million (UK, 144 million); Soviet bloc, 710 million; Latin America, 240 million; South-East Asia, 200 million; Africa, 95 million.

'These figures are based on projections of how international oil requirements for industry, motor transport, domestic heating and the chemical industry are likely to grow.

'They allow for the enormous expected growth of air traffic (currently about 12 per cent per year) but cannot take account of the further vast increase that would be occasioned by a switch to supersonics, whose production still requires British and American Government approval.

'The critical factor is that the supersonics consume up to two-and-a-half times as much fuel per passenger-mile as subsonic aircraft, and are ultimately expected to carry about 20 per cent of all traffic. In 1990, for example, there are expected to be 600 transatlantic crossings a day by supersonics, compared with 200 by subsonic airliners if the latter are all "jumbo"-sized jets.

'To meet increased demand, the oil industry is currently planning to double its production in the next decade – from a world total of about 2,000 million tons this year to 4,100 million tons in 1980.

'Tanker tonnage, refinery capacity and well-head production must double in the next ten years to meet these demands. Whether the oil industry can do this is doubtful.

'By 1985, the combined Boeing and Concorde fleets will need around 11 per cent of currently projected world oil demand, and very much more than the requirements of several underdeveloped continents.

'All this suggests that the £2,000m that will ultimately be needed to launch the Concorde and the Boeing could be more rationally applied to the development of technologies that will ease, not aggravate, the transition to a world without oil.' *The Observer*, 30th August, 1970.

Pollution near Airports

At take-off the Boeing SST would burn about one ton of fuel each minute – far more than subsonic jets burn. The amounts of toxic pollutants inflicted on the nearby downwind communities would be large. Already the people in such communities find such pollution a major annoyance.

Nor is this merely a matter of pollution by partly-burnt kerosene. The fuel systems of aircraft provide very suitable environments for the growth of certain bacteria and yeasts, which cause corrosion and blockages. To prevent the growth of these organisms, various antibiotics are added to the fuel. Some of these are metallic-based; others are based on phenols; many of them are listed as highly dangerous industrial poisons. It is sometimes assumed that these substances are rendered harmless by passing through the engines, but where fuel is incompletely combusted, some of the additives emerge unaltered. Some of these additives are capable of emerging from the combustion process in a state as dangerous as when they went in.

The problem of poisonous fuel additives is of course not restricted to the vicinity of airports – these additives have now achieved world-wide distribution by 'fallout'.

Effects on animals

It is certain that the SSTs' repeated sonic bangs would annoy many kinds of animals. It is *possible* that harmful long-term effects will occur also. There are already many instances in which bangs from military planes have caused horses and cows to panic. In Switzerland a herd of prize cattle stampeded over a cliff when frightened by a sonic bang (*National Parks Magazine*, March 1968), and it is also reported that in France a horse was startled by a bang and ran away, throwing and killing the rider.[2] At the Edwards Air Force Base sonic bang tests, several horses exhibited fright symptoms.

Mink are especially vulnerable. In 1966, sonic bangs from Air Force F-101 jet planes resulted in the death of approximately 2,000 baby mink on the farm of Mr Z. Taylor of Frazee, Minnesota, according to a finding by the Federal District Court in St Paul on 29th June, 1968. Mr Taylor was awarded $37,490 damages (*North Shore News*, Bothell, Washington, 11th September, 1968). Mink ranchers in Minnesota testified that when sonic bangs struck their farms, the female mink '. . . jumped from their boxes, then bounced back into the boxes again. Dead mink kits were found in the boxes and cages afterwards, some of them partially devoured.

Sonic bang tests carried out on mink farms in Virginia in 1967 by the US Department of Agriculture showed that even relatively mild simulated sonic bangs (average overpressure 1.0 lb/sq. ft) inflicted on whelping female mink throughout the whelping period resulted in doubling the mortality rate of the baby mink. The mortality rate was 15.5 per cent, as compared to 7.2 per cent for the control group (ref. 96).

Chickens and turkeys are startled by sonic bangs. A farmer in Hallock, Minnesota, was paid $50 because bangs caused his chickens to panic and suffocate against a wall (ref. 83).

2. SST & Sonic Boom handbook, W. A. Shurcliff, 1970, ref. 70.

Sonic bangs may have disastrous effects on colonies of birds that nest on cliffs – because bangs make the birds fly off so impetuously that they knock their eggs out of the nest and the eggs then roll or fall and are soon broken. Likewise, eggs can be knocked out of nests in trees. Mass breakage of eggs after sudden loud noises is already well known, according to A. H. Morgan, Executive Vice-President, Massachusetts Audubon Society (letter of 7th December, 1968).

On 24th September, 1970, *New Scientist* (London) reported:

> 'The closely protected Dry Tortugas colony of sooty terns (*Sterns fuscata*) and brown noddies (*Anous stolidus*) has enjoyed a phenomenal breeding success for more than fifty years. In 1969 the birds returned in their usual numbers (some 50,000 pairs of sooties and 2,500 pairs of noddies) in early April, and laid eggs, and started incubating normally. However, when O. L. Austin and W. B. Robertson, of Florida State Museum, and G. E. Wolfenden, South Florida University, arrived to ring the young in mid-June, instead of the usual hordes of sooty chicks they found almost none. About half the normal number of adults were still present, but markedly wild and restless. Apparently only a few of the earliest-laid eggs had hatched, a very few were still being incubated, and the rest were deserted – most contained dead, partly grown embryos. Only 242 sooty chicks were ringed instead of the usual 25,000. The noddies, on the other hand, had bred normally.
>
> What made the sooty eggs fail halfway through incubation is still somewhat uncertain, reported the scientists in a paper read to the 15th International Ornithological Congress in The Hague earlier this month. There had been no weather abnormalities, no shortage of food in the neighbouring waters, no disturbance by natural predators or by human visitors to the island. Laboratory examination of eggs, chicks, and adult tissues showed low pesticide residues.
>
> The only unusual elements were: dense vegetation,

which made it difficult for the sooties to reach their nests in the more populous sectors; and frequent sonic booms from jet planes breaking the sound barrier. The booms were strong enough to shatter windows on the adjoining Garden Key. The birds had reacted to the occasional sonic booms of the previous season by rising immediately in a panic flight, circling over the island momentarily, and then usually settling down on their eggs again. While there is no evidence that sonic booms caused physical damage to the eggs, it is entirely possible that they occurred often enough to disturb the sooties' incubating rhythm and thereby caused desertion.

Action has been taken to curb jet booms, within range of the Tortugas, and much excess vegetation cleared. Thus the 1970 season appears to have progressed normally.'

USA and Canadian experts on fish ecology have stated that virtually nothing is known as to whether, or how much, sonic bangs might affect fish. It is well known that only an extremely small fraction of the shock-wave energy would enter the water, but even this small amount, striking during periods of quiet, might be expected to alarm fish. Fishermen have reported seeing fish – startled by a sonic bang – jump out of the water and then lie on their sides, as if stunned (ref. 23, p. 21, 1). The US Department of the Interior has planned sonic bang tests on fish off the coast of California, but it is hard to see how the bangs could be violent enough, and continued throughout a long enough period to represent fairly the long-term disturbance of a fleet of transoceanic SSTs.

The suggestion that sonic bangs could disturb fish is discounted by some, who argue that the overpressure in the shock wave is insignificant compared to the various pressures to which fish are subjected. But this – like the comparison of the bang to a 35 mph wind (see Chapter Five) ignores the fact that the bang is both violent and sudden; if fish are stunned, this may be the reason.

The supersonic testing of Concorde 002 has produced a

very large number of reports of the response of animals to the sonic bangs: cows collapsing or stampeding, ponies bolting, sheep panicking, chickens becoming 'hysterical', flocks of wild birds taking-off in alarm.

Degradation of mountain and moorland areas, National parks, etc.

US Secretary of Transportation Alan S. Boyd, testifying before a Congressional Committee on 22nd May, 1967, said that even if SSTs could not be permitted to fly over densely populated regions (because of the sonic bang), routes over thinly populated areas could probably be worked out. He suggested, for example, that supersonic flights could be permitted between Chicago and the West Coast – an area containing plains, mountains, and few people. Special effort would be made, he implied, to establish SST supersonic routes over such wilderness areas.

Similarly in the UK, the distinction is made between overflying areas of dense population and overflying areas of sparse population and wilderness.

But does this make sense? C. Edward Graves, naturalist and writer, says in the Winter 1967–8 *Living Wilderness* (ref. 36):

> 'Imagine a hike or a pack trip into the wildest part of the country in order to enjoy its peculiar characteristics, only to have the quiet of an evening campfire shattered by cannonading booms from the sky! Their unexpectedness is one of the worst features. Tranquillity would no longer exist. The nerve-shattering impact upon man, and the harassment to wildlife through constant exposure to the sonic boom, are incalculable.'

In the USA there have been many protests from hikers and campers who have *already* had their national-park vacations spoiled by repeated, explosion-like sonic bangs from military planes. If SSTs too were allowed to fly at supersonic speed over parks, the number of bangs would increase a hundredfold.

In the UK, sonic bangs in the early days of military supersonic flying produced such a strong public reaction that such flying has been confined, for many years, to over the sea. It is for this reason that the British public is far less aware than are US citizens of the effects of supersonic flight.

Are over-the-ocean supersonic flights acceptable?

Proponents of the SST regard it as obvious that supersonic flights over oceans are acceptable. The oceans are practically devoid of people, they say; therefore sonic bangs present no problems.

Mr B. K. O. Lundberg, however, has insisted for some years that routine SST operations over the sea would not be acceptable. Mr Lundberg analysed the available information and summarized it in his 1968 60-page report 'Acceptable Nominal Sonic Boom Overpressure in SST Operation Over Land and Sea' (ref. 58), and again in 'The Economy and Sonic Boom of the Sea-limited SST' (August 1970).

Let us list some of the main facts. The greatest concentrations of SST supersonic routes would be over the North Atlantic, between USA and Europe. An SST would produce especially intense bangs when carrying an almost full load of fuel during first acceleration above Mach. 1; at this time of maximum bang the plane would be just off the coast. But it is here that the greatest concentrations of freighters, tankers, passenger ships, fishing vessels, and pleasure vessels is highest. Persons on such ships must expect as many as one or two sonic bangs per hour, day and night. Worse, they must expect occasional super-bangs in the overpressure range 4.0 to 8.0 psf.

Multiple reflections of the bang shock-wave from ship superstructures can produce further increase in overpressure. Already investigators of sonic bang effects have observed breakage of a ship's thick plate glass window by a bang that had an estimated overpressure of about 6 psf (*The Times*, October 1960) (also ref. 60).

It has been estimated that each SST flight across the

North Atlantic would subject about 4,000 persons (on average) to sonic bangs.

It is likely that shipowners will object to such treatment and that, similarly, crew members will object to being treated as second-class citizens by being subjected to repeated bangs considered too severe to be inflicted on people on land.

A considerable area of the North Atlantic would be struck by sonic bangs – partly because the east-bound routes and west-bound routes would be spaced about 100 miles apart, and partly because the SSTs would be serving widely scattered cities in the eastern USA and Canada and equally widely scattered cities in Europe. Bang-zone maps published in the July 1967 *Space Aeronautics* suggest that about 80 per cent of the area of the North Atlantic bounded by lines drawn from Newfoundland to Ireland and from New York to Portugal would be blanketed by bangs. Keeping the SSTs and ships on well-separated, parallel courses is out of the question because of the many departure points and many destinations of ships as well as SSTs.

Yachtsmen, too, may be expected to protest. On 18th July, 1969, the US Citizens' League Against the Sonic Boom released a list of 118 prominent yachtsmen whose objections to coastal sonic bangs had been conveyed to President Nixon. Each of the 118 yachtsmen had signed a petition reading:

> 'As one who frequents coastal waters of USA, I oppose using these waters as a dumping-ground for sonic booms from SSTs and I respectfully request government authorities to do their best to prevent this degradation of the environment.
>
> Should the airlines proceed to inflict sonic booms routinely on these waters, in disregard to my rights there, I will consider taking appropriate legal action to protect those rights.'

Prominent British yachtsmen have not, as yet, taken similar action.

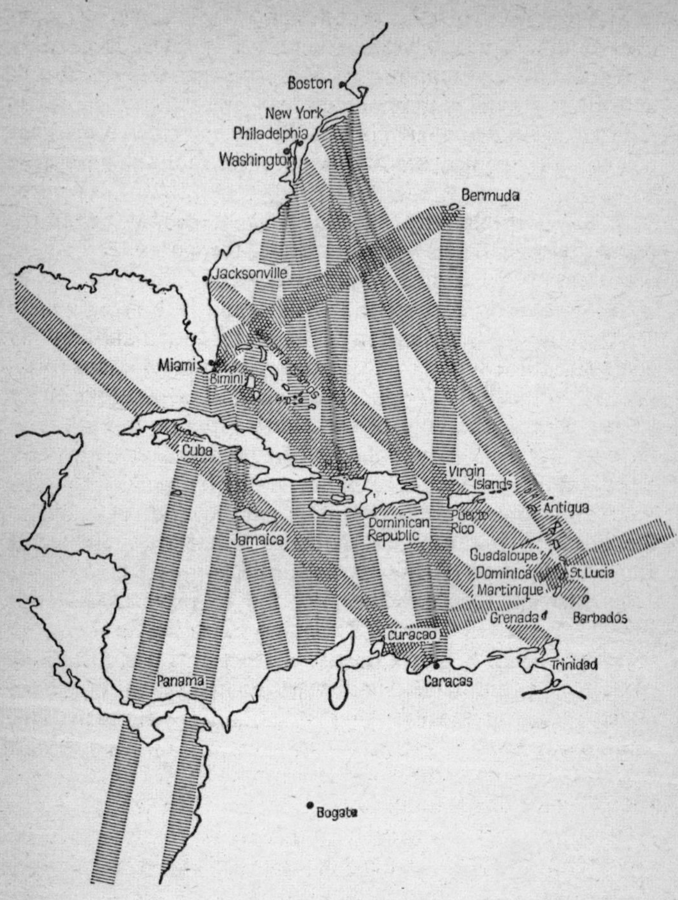

Fig. 7. Map showing the bang-paths of possible supersonic routes over the Caribbean area.

If the reason for the prohibition of SSTs overflying the mainland is that they would otherwise disrupt the lives of the mainland inhabitants, then it is logical that the ban should extend to overflying inhabited islands. However, for the SSTs to circumvent islands is often not feasible – if adjacent islands are less than fifty miles apart (because the bang-zone is about fifty miles wide) and form long chains. The 900-mile-long east-west chain of Caribbean islands, for example, would block a majority of the direct routes from the eastern US to South America. (See Figure 7.)

It has been argued that SSTs such as the Concorde could fly into and out of Europe at supersonic speeds along the English Channel, but we have yet to see a map showing the east-bound and west-bound flight paths, each with a bang-zone fifty miles wide, and separated laterally by whatever distance air traffic control would require, all superimposed upon the English Channel – which in part is only 22 miles wide.

Mr Angus Maude, MP, a former Conservative aviation spokesman, wrote in the *Spectator* on 7th March, 1969, in an article entitled 'In defence of the Concorde' (Mr Maude was defending it against the attacks contained in the Anti-Concorde Project's full-page advertisement in the *Guardian*, 10th February, 1969): 'The odds are that Concorde's supersonic flight will be (and ought to be) banned over inhabited land *and main shipping routes*' [our italics]. Mr Maude went on to assert that 'Concorde *could* still prove a commercial success even with the ban' [his italics]. Mr Maude's belief that Concorde could achieve commercial success in these circumstances appears to be singularly inconsistent with the facts.

The cost of environmental conservation

The cost-benefit analysis of the Concorde project by Mr C. B. Edwards was regarded by BAC as 'a fair assessment' (please see Chapter 8 – The Cost of Concorde). Significantly (although it is doubtful whether the significance was realized by BAC) they went on to argue that 'it is an economist's view and there are some things that cannot just be judged in book-keeping terms'. This statement provides the fulcrum on which to balance the advantages and disadvantages of continuing with the Concorde Project.

The development of the Concorde has channelled vast amounts of government money – taxpayers' money – to the contractors and subcontractors. While the project continues, these benefits continue. But the project cannot conceivably be profitable in any normal sense, as most (and probably all) of the cost of development (which may reach £1,000m) is irrecoverable. Claims are made that Concorde has brought much technological 'spin-off' – but these claims are vague, and are usually highly exaggerated. The claim that Concorde will bring 'prestige' is equally dubious.

As BAC suggests, there are many factors not readily convertible into 'book-keeping terms'. If fleets of Concordes were put into operation, their supersonic flight – over mainland areas, islands, 'sparsely-populated areas', or shipping lanes – would subject people, buildings, and wild life to frequent and (to say the least) undesirable sonic bangs. At airports, SSTs would produce noise far in excess of present levels – intolerable though these are.

Bad environmental effects of this type are of course not confined to supersonic airliners. Other examples are the accumulation of oil and sewage on coastlines, the contamination of lakes and rivers, the effects of mining in national parks, traffic congestion, air pollution. It is not easy to quantify these bad effects, or 'spillovers' as they are coming to be called, in 'book-keeping terms'. But another economist, Dr E. J. Mishan, has described how this could be attempted:[3] 'When these noxious by-products of industry or of industrial goods are thrown off, segments of the public are constrained to absorb them without compensation. A topical example is air travel which produces services for the passengers while simultaneously producing simultaneous disservices, aircraft noise, for large numbers of the population . . . Once the costs associated with adverse spillover

3. Dr E. J. Mishan: 'The Spillover Enemy – the coming struggle for amenity rights' in *Encounter*, Dec. 1969.

effects are a charge on the production costs of the perpetrators of spillovers, then, unless they can reach agreement with the affected groups, they have to desist entirely from producing the spillover-generating goods. Thus an airline company would have the option of continuing all its services provided completely effective anti-noise devices were installed, or, to the extent that they were not completely effective, of paying full compensation for all the residual noise thrown on to the public. Under such a dispensation the costs of operating the Concorde over Britain would have to include compensation for inflicting on us a plague of sonic booms. As an economic proposition it would be a dead duck.'

That the operation of aircraft such as the Concorde would disrupt people's lives and cause annoyance and suffering is inevitable. That repeated sonic bangs would destroy the peace in many wild places is certain. But what price peace and quiet? That vast fleets of SSTs, flying in the stratosphere, might induce increased cloud cover is possible. What price sunlight? That the vast amounts of fuel required by these fleets of SSTs could be put to better use is obvious. It is equally clear that the immense financial investments involved in the SST projects could have been used to tackle pressing social and environmental problems – and to develop quieter, safer and cheaper air travel. Environmentalists have frequently been told: 'If you want to conserve the environment then you've got to pay the cost.' For too long this assertion, and the assumptions that underlie it, have gone almost unchallenged. The environmentalists must reply by insisting upon the adoption of practical ecologically-based methods by which to judge the full effects and the full cost of our actions – including technological developments.

Supersonic transport versus environmental conservation is something of a test case.

CHAPTER EIGHT

The Cost of Concorde

In his 'Concorde – a case study in cost-benefit analysis',[1] Mr C. B. Edwards summarizes the history of cost escalation in the Concorde project:

'In November 1962, the Franco-British Concorde agreement was signed – at about the same time as Edward Heath was negotiating for Britain to enter the European Economic Community.

'In January 1963, General de Gaulle shattered Britain's immediate hopes of entering the Common Market and the "Tories were left with a deeply political aircraft whose deeply political *raison d'être* had been knocked from under it" (ref. 72).

'At the time when the agreement was signed, no detailed specification of any kind existed either for the aircraft or for the manufacturing programme, and the cost estimates were, as Sir Richard Way, Permanent Secretary to the Ministry of Aviation, told the Public Accounts Committee "really arbitrary . . . not a great deal more than an inspired guess". (Public Accounts Committee, November 1962.)

'In 1962, the estimated total cost of developing the aircraft to the production stage was about £150m to £170m.

'In 1963 the House of Commons Estimates Committee looked at the agreement and found that the Treasury had never authorized the project, had played *no* part in preparing the agreement and were *not* represented on the Concorde Directing Committee. (House of Commons Estimates Committee, 1963. Quoted in ref. 72). In 1964 there was a change of Government in the UK and in October 1964 the

1. 'Concorde – a case study in cost-benefit analysis' by C. B Edwards, Lecturer in Economics, University of East Anglia. July 1969. Revised October 1970 (ref. 31).

"Brown Paper" stated that: "The Government have already communicated to the French Government their wish to re-examine urgently the Concorde project" (ref. 29). There was, however, found to be no breach clause in the agreement and it was suggested that the French could have collected more than £100m damages from the British if the latter had unilaterally terminated the contract.

'In May 1965 major design changes were announced, and since the major contracts had been drawn up on a cost-plus and price-to-be-agreed basis with no incentive arrangements the estimate of the cost to the Governments rose from £280m in 1964 to £500m in 1966 (ref. 32). Meanwhile, in April 1966, BAC had written to the Ministry of Aviation stating that there was no question of its putting any of its own capital at risk in Concorde (ref. 2). The Public Accounts Committee report in 1966 carpeted the Treasury and the Ministry of Aviation for allowing costs to soar, failing to check cost sharing between the two countries, or to give contractors incentives (ref. 32).

'But still the estimated research and development costs continued to rise. In 1969, the cost estimate for research and development was given as £730m, with *no* provision for "contingencies", and on 10th November, 1969, the Minister of Technology told the House of Commons that the agreed Anglo-French estimate of £730m was being revised to take account of the devaluation of the franc and certain adjustments to the programme. Earlier in May 1969 the Minister of Technology had proposed a research and development cost limit of £840m, but it is likely that the total research and development costs to the production stage will be around £1,000m (ref. 63).

'In July 1970, following the change in Government in the UK the new Minister of Technology, Mr Geoffrey Rippon, was reported as saying that £240m had already been spent on development by *each* country, leaving at least another £125m to be found by each country if the latest budget was to be adhered to (ref. 33).'

The latest statement on Concorde was made on 28th October, 1970:

'Mr Corfield, Minister of Aviation Supply (Gloucestershire, South, C.), replying to questions on the progress of test flights of the Concorde, said: "Concorde's flight tests are continuing to make satisfactory progress. We shall review the project thoroughly, in consultation with the French Government, in the light of the results of the current series of tests and the commercial prospects of the aircraft.

"The latest estimate of development cost is £825m at June 1970 prices." (Some cries of "Oh".)

He also issued the following written statement on the development costs of Concorde. It said:

The latest basic estimate of £825m is divided as follows as between actual past expenditure and estimated future expenditure:

Actual costs from 29th November, 1962, to 30th September, 1970, at the prices and exchange rates prevailing when the costs were incurred: British Government, £240m; French Government £220m; both Governments, £460m.

Estimated costs from 30th September, 1970, to completion of the programme at June 1970 prices and an exchange rate of £1 = 13.33 Fr. – British Government £165m; French Government £200m; both Governments £365m.

Totals: British Government, £405m; French Government £420m; both Governments, £825m.

'One cannot expect the airlines to enter into firm commitments until the manufacturer is in a position to give a firm undertaking about performance of the aircraft which they cannot do until after the tests. I would envisage probably March or April next year.'

(*Hansard*, 28th October, 1970, also reported in *The Times*, 29th October.)

Mr Edwards discusses the arguments which have been put forward in favour of Concorde – the claimed favourable effects upon the balance of payments; technological 'fallout'; prestige; employment creation, etc. This section is extensively quoted in Chapter 9, Facts and Fallacies. Mr Edwards then considers the question: 'Should the Concorde be cancelled now?':

'What then are the likely net benefits or costs of abandoning Concorde now that something like £500m has been spent on research and development, but a further £400m is to be spent on development and something like £100m is likely to be spent on jigging and tooling? One could calculate the net benefits or costs either by "discounting"[2] the costs and benefits to, say, 1980 back to a "present value" or by accumulating interest to 1980 on the cumulative amount spent. It is more appropriate to accumulate interest on the outstanding capital because this is more likely to be understood. But what rate of interest should we use? One argument has it that since this is the Government getting money from the Government, a nil rate of interest should be used. The objection to this argument is obvious. The alternative to spending the money on Concorde is to spend the money on schools, hospitals, social security, or even on a European airbus project. These alternatives would generate benefits for the British economy. But at what rate? This is not known but it seems reasonable to take the rate which the Treasury uses when evaluating expenditure proposals by the Nationalized Industries in the UK, namely 8 per cent per annum.

If we assume:

(i) a future pre-production expenditure by the two Governments of £500m during the period 1971 to 1973;[3]

2. 'Discounting' is simply a procedure for attaching lower weights to costs and benefits which occur in the more distant future than to those which occur relatively soon. If £1.0 is worth £1.1 in a year from now at a 10 per cent per annum rate of interest, the £1.1 receivable a year from now has a 'present' or 'discounted' value today of £1.0 using the same rate of interest.

3. And therefore forget about the past expenditure of £500m, since

(ii) an "optimistic" production profit of about £2m aircraft (including spares);[4] and

(iii) a "very optimistic" sales figure of 200 aircraft from 1973 to 1980, or about 25 a year;

– the loss to 1980 would be as follows:

– that is about £444m or, assuming the cost is shared equally between the two Governments, a loss to the UK alone of over £220m.

If a more realistic sales figure to 1980 of 100 aircraft is assumed, then the loss (including interest) to 1980 to the British economy would be about £340m;[5] and, of course, if the operating surplus per aircraft were less than £2m, then the loss would be even greater.

It is, of course, quite possible that if the project were now abandoned, there would be considerable short-term unemployment, especially in the SW of England. But it is unlikely that there would be a long-term employment problem arising from a cancellation of the project. The Plowden Report stated that it had heard evidence on the redundancies after the cancellation of the TSR2 and that this led them "to believe that in general new jobs would fairly quickly be found for aircraft labour if it were released".[6] The Report was written in 1965 but ex-Concorde workers are unlikely to find much difficulty in obtaining

---

even if we cancel Concorde now, we will have lost the £500m already spent.

4. Even now (in 1970) the estimates for the production costs are not known with any accuracy and nor are the likely average prices of the aircraft or its spares, but we optimistically assume here that the profit per aircraft is estimated at about £1m, represented by a sales price of £9m and production costs of £8m and that for each aircraft the sales of spares (costing £3m to produce) brings in about £4m.

5. This assumes following Sturmey (ref. 87) that the production cost would be constant and therefore the average profit per aircraft would still be £2m. Sturmey's article in the *Economic Journal* 1964 suggested that the variation in average cost per aircraft varies very little with the number of aircraft produced (between 80 and 200 per annum) once development costs and jigging and tooling costs are excluded.

6. Report of the Committee of Inquiry into Aircraft Industry, 1964–65, Table II, Appendix C (Plowden Report).

Comparative scale of losses 1971–1980

Year	*(Annual Expenditure)*	*Net Income from Sales*	*Cummulative Income (Expenditure) Before Interest*	*8% p.a. Interest*	*Cumulative Income (Expenditure)*
	£m	£m	£m	£m	£m
1971	(170)	—	(170)	(14)	(184)
72	(170)	—	(354)	(28)	(382)
73	(170)	50	(502)	(40)	(542)
74	—	50	(492)	(39)	(531)
75	—	50	(481)	(38)	(519)
76	—	50	(469)	(37)	(506)
77	—	50	(456)	(36)	(492)
78	—	50	(442)	(35)	(477)
79	—	50	(427)	(34)	(461)
80	—	50	(411)	(33)	(444)

new jobs. There is, according to figures produced by the Department of Employment and Productivity, no shortage of professional and scientific jobs in the South West; on the other hand the unemployment of semi-skilled and unskilled workers is difficult to predict if the project were cancelled in 1970. There could be a substanial adjustment problem in the South West where (in June 1964) about 12 per cent of the total manufacturing employment was in the aircraft industry. A substantial part of Concorde's employment is in the Filton (near Bristol) division of BAC and the Bristol factories of Bristol Siddeley Engines (Rolls-Royce) but because of sub-contracting the likely employment effect is difficult to predict exactly. However, if we assume that the total direct employment on Concorde in the UK is about 25,000, then if compensation of £1,000 per employee were paid representing, say, six months' pay for six months' unemployment, then the cost to the economy would be £25m at the most. *Thus even taking assumptions which are favourable to Concorde* (high production profits per aircraft, high "dislocation" costs, large sales, no further delays) *the British economy would save £200m by cancelling the project now.*'

This figure relates to future costs only – it assumes that the money spent to 1970 is written-off as irrecoverable. Mr Edwards points out that the figure does not include the cost of damage, disturbance, and other ill-effects resulting from sonic bangs, airport noise or other undesirable 'spillovers'. (Please see Chapter 7.)

A diagram showing the rising estimates of the cost of Concorde, and the loss that would result from a 'successful' outcome of the project, is reprinted on pages 102–3. This diagram formed part of the Anti-Concorde Project's full-page advertisement in *The Times*, 18th May, 1970. It is based upon the 'optimistic' assumptions referred to by Mr Edwards: 200 aircraft sold; manufacturing costs of £11m each; selling price £13m (both figures including spare parts).

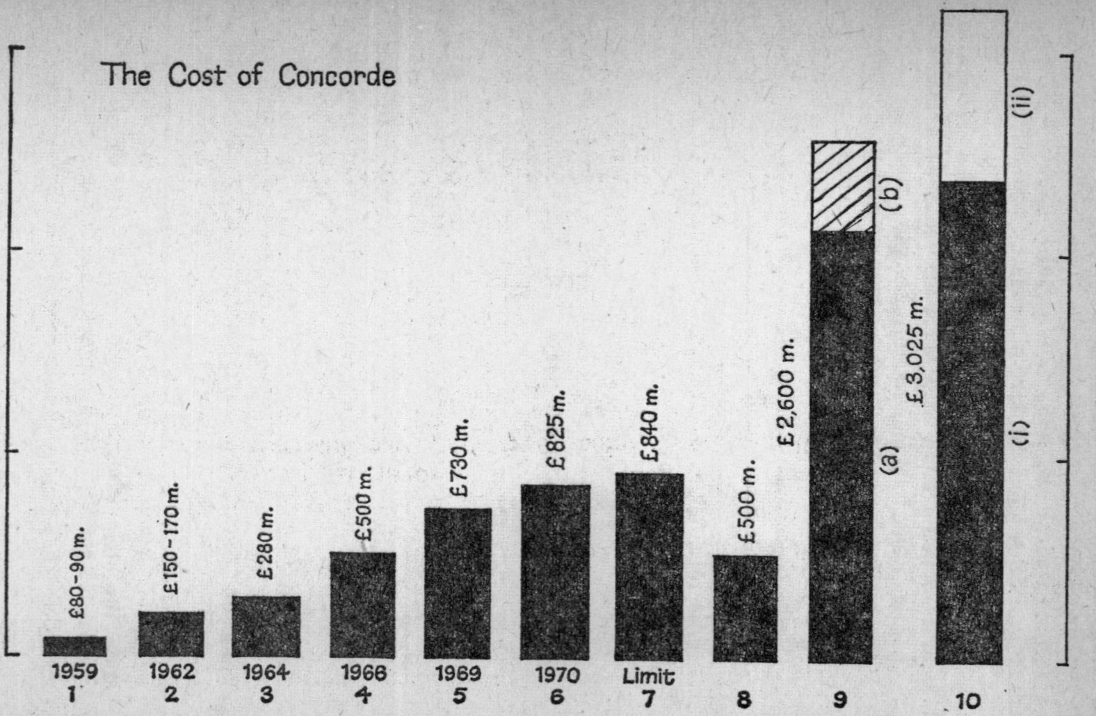
The Cost of Concorde
£80-90 m.
£150-170 m.
£280 m.
£500 m.
£730 m.
£825 m.
£840 m.
£500 m.
£2,600 m.
(a)
(b)
£3,025 m.
(i)
(ii)
1959
1
1962
2
1964
3
1966
4
1969
5
1970
6
Limit
7
8
9
10

(1 to 5) Progressive estimates of the cost of research and development for Concorde.

(1) Estimate for the Supersonic Transport Aircraft Committee (1959).

(2) Estimate at the time of the Anglo-French Concorde Agreement (1962).

(3 to 6) Subsequent revised estimates. The 1969 estimate *excludes* the cost of establishing the production line and a reserve for "contingencies" – both included in some previous estimates. (Production line financing now estimated at £200m.)! **The research and development costs are now admitted to be largely or entirely irrecoverable.**

(7) The cost limit proposed by the Minister of Technology in May 1969.

(8) The amount already spent (late 1970).

(9 & 10) The result of a "successful" outcome of the Concorde project (with 200 machines sold) showing.

(9) Selling price (Incl. spares) :	**£2,600m.**
(a) Production costs :	£2,200m.
(b) Manufacturers' profits :	£400m.
(10) Total costs :	**£3,200m.**
(i) Production costs :[1]	£2,200m.
(ii) Pre-production costs (irrecoverable – therefore a loss to British and French governments and people) :	£1,000m.

The figures in (9) and (10) are probably biased in favour of the Concorde. Higher costs for development or production, or lower profits or sales figures, would of course increase the loss.

1. Recent estimates of the cost of establishing the production line: £300m.

CHAPTER NINE

Facts and Fallacies

In an analysis of the viability of supersonic transport, certain factors emerge which are worthy of comment. Often it is the most frequently voiced claims which go unexamined. Certain of these claims are justified; many of them are fallacious.

Time-saving fallacy

One oft-repeated claim is that SST 'will cut travel times by half'. That this is far from the truth is shown by the diagram below (Fig. 8).

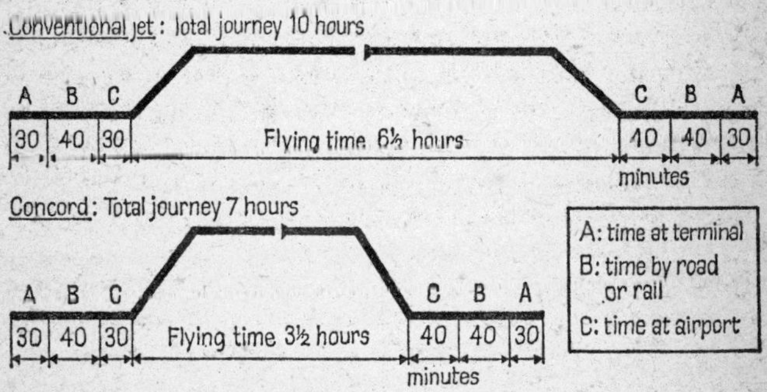

Comparative journey times – subsonic and supersonic. Based on Fig. 1.1 in ref. 9a.

On favourable assumptions – no unusual delays at take-off[1] or landing or during the ground sectors of the journey,

1. If a technical fault were to develop in an SST prior to take-off, a very long delay might ensue since, owing to the high cost of these aircraft, it is unlikely that many standby planes will be available.

If the arrangements for one-class (first class) Concordes and one class (tourist) subsonics – proposed recently by the makers of Concorde for example – a transatlantic journey using a subsonic jet gives a total journey time (city centre to city centre) of about ten hours. On the same assumptions travel by Concorde would reduce this to about seven hours. The US SST – even with its higher cruising speed – would cut the time only ten minutes below Concorde. The time-saving achieved by supersonic travel is less than one-third.

Far fewer than 1 per cent of the people of even the wealthiest nations are regular travellers on inter-continental flights – and only a fraction of these would travel by Concorde. Incomparably greater savings of time and increases of efficiency, benefiting immensely greater numbers of people, could be obtained by spending a small proportion of the cost of SST projects on (for example) improving the increasingly inadequate and chaotic conditions of public transport on the ground. Even comparatively limited improvements in transport between airports and city-centres (perhaps with Customs and formalities carried out en route) would result in large time-savings for all air travellers.

Even the simplest exercise in cost benefit analysis reveals that while the 100 supersonic passengers were saving two or three hours each (say 300 man-hours) on the flight, the time wasted by disturbance of people on the ground by sonic bang would exceed this by a factor of hundreds or thousands.

In the early days of SST advocacy it was assumed that SSTs would be given priority at airports (the supposed justification for this is not clear). This hope has had to be abandoned; it is now admitted that SSTs would have to join the queues of aircraft waiting in stacking areas for their turn to land.

Day-trips to New York

There has been much talk about 'day-trips across the Atlantic in the supersonic era' – more talk, in fact, than

---

were adopted, then in the event of Concorde being prevented from taking off by some technical fault, the first class Concorde passengers could find themselves compelled to travel not only subsonically but also tourist class.

thought. Such a trip would involve seven hours (minimum) flying – and total journey times *between city centres* amounting probably to 14 hours. If the traveller's starting-point, transatlantic destination, and finishing-point were some distance from the air terminal, more travelling time would be involved. Day-trips to Europe from the USA are an especially dubious proposition. A businessman making an early start from New York – having got up in time to be at the airport for the take-off at 09.00 – would arrive in London at around 19.00 (London time). Presumably he would have travelled in order to work and not merely to dine, and his hosts would be willing to prolong their working day well into the night. To return to New York by midnight (to preserve the concept of a day-trip) it would be necessary to take off by 01.30 (London time) – waking the inhabitants of the western areas of London in the process.

On a typical SST flight, most passengers will get no sleep. On night-time flights this will be a major embarrassment. Consider a traveller who leaves New York at 23.00 bound for London. He will reach his hotel in London at about 03.30 New York time, which is 08.30 London time – just as the working day there begins. But he will have had no sleep!

It is impractical to give up such night-time flights and fly the Atlantic just during the day, not only because the traveller then wastes the better part of the day en route, but also because the small chance that SST operation might be profitable disappears entirely unless the SSTs are kept in use almost constantly.

To what extent do businessmen want or need supersonic travel?

One businessman gave his views to the *Daily Telegraph* (18th October, 1970):

> 'With his experience of flying, Mr Jock Gordon, export director for Lines Bros., the toy manufacturers, well qualifies as a spokesman for his colleagues.
>
> "The main thing I, and most businessmen want, is

comfort. Sheer speed, certainly on long distance flights, is not so vital. Thus, I see no advantage in the Concorde. There can be very few cases where getting to New York in nearly half the time is that important. You can always telephone." '

Time-zone fatigue

The fact that rapid crossing of many time-zones produces a state of fatigue is becoming increasingly well-known. This fatigue results from interference with the body's circadian rhythms.

Long-distance SST trips across time-zones will give the traveller little chance to adjust his 'biological clock', or circadian rhythm. Many kinds of biological and psychological disruptions may occur (*Science*, 13th June, 1969, p. 1288). Representatives of governments and corporations who fly from continent to continent are not allowed to make a major decision until after they have spent 48 hours in the country of arrival. 'Air travellers who cross the . . . Pacific . . . generally suffer a desynchronization of certain biological rhythms. Their timing mechanism goes awry' (*Parade*, 14th January, 1968, p. 20). Dr S. R. Mohler, Chief of Medical Applications, FAA, says '. . . allow one or two days' acclimatization before taking part in demanding activities . . .' Thus the primary benefit of the SST – the saving in time – is diminished.

Although an SST flight would take less time than a subsonic journey over the same route, it would do so at the price of several discomforts. Failure to rest and recuperate brings the risk that the executive might miss some implication in the discussion or in the 'small print' and commit some error which would be impossible or difficult to put right. In this context the time saved by supersonic travel is without significance: the traveller may arrive even more weary than after a more restful subsonic flight, and if he were subsequently to spend two days resting nothing would be gained.

Faster forms of communication
A direct-dialling transatlantic telephone service is currently being established. This service may spread until it is worldwide. With loud-speaking telephones and television link-up added, there will be little incentive for supersonic day-trips to New York.

Demand fallacy

The supposed demand for supersonic travel, and the supposed market for supersonic airliners, have been based upon several identifiable fallacies. Two of these, in turn, are founded upon insufficient understanding of the nature of exponential growth. The first of these is the frequently repeated claim that because (since the industrial revolution) the speeds at which people have been able to travel have become faster and faster, *therefore* we shall and inevitably must travel ever faster. The second is the famous graph showing the increase in numbers of people travelling by air.

World air passenger traffic (excluding Russia and China) has increased steadily since 1945. Throughout the early 1960s the increase was about 12½ per cent per year. In 1965 the number of passengers was 177 million. An annual growth rate of 12½ per cent means that the total is doubled every six years. Some have assumed that this rate of increase would continue indefinitely, and that a substantial proportion of these vast numbers of people would travel in SSTs. But this growth rate would produce a total of more than 1,000 millions in 1980; 2,000 millions in 1986; 4,000 millions in 1992.

The absurdity of these figures is clear, and of course the pro-SST people do not take their graphs so far. They take them just far enough to show, to their own satisfaction, a 'vast potential' market for SSTs in the years when, it is proposed, SSTs should be becoming available. But even a small reduction in the actual rate of growth makes a large difference to the figure achieved after a few years.

It is in the nature of such exponential growth rates that they slow down, and currently the rates of growth of air traffic are doing just that. An IATA paper published in 1967[2] postulated growth rates of just over 10 per cent for 1970 to 1975, and just under 10 per cent for 1975 to 1980. This produces a figure of 768 million for 1980 (compared to more than 1,000 million on the assumption of 12½ per cent annual growth). More recently it has become apparent that the actual future growth rates are likely to be lower than the 1967 estimates. It is already recognized that world airlines have too many aircraft. Load factors (the percentage of seats that are occupied) are low; profits are low or non-existent.

The jumbo-jets have been developed, built and introduced into operation while the SSTs have been gestating. They are a formidable new form of competition – vastly more spacious and comfortable than the Concorde; quicker than other subsonic aircraft; they have far greater range than Concorde (or other SSTs) and of course are not subject to sonic bang restrictions.

Supersonic travel is inherently more expensive than subsonic. Unless there is a dramatic and unexpected increase in air travel at first-class prices on transoceanic routes, airlines contemplating buying Concordes might face these options: (i) to raise fares on their 'jumbos' to subsidize the Concordes – and reduce the number of jumbo passengers; (ii) to buy Concordes for 'prestige' and fly them at a vast loss; (iii) to force down the selling price of Concorde to a 'giveaway' level – thereby reducing their operating losses.

Employment creation fallacy

It is argued that the Concorde Project is important in the creation of employment for many thousands, and that cancellation of the project would be detrimental in that it will put people out of work.

The total direct employment on Concorde in the UK is probably no more than 25,000. A very large proportion of these are skilled professional and technical workers with pre-

2. John Davis, *The Concorde Affair*, p. 205.

cisely those skills which have been, and still are in short supply in the UK.

'In 1965 the Plowden Committee of Inquiry into the Aircraft industry said that "... for the kind of workers employed in the aircraft industry it is not jobs, but men that are scarce" (para. 154) and it went on to say (in para. 156) that "Our general conclusion is that no case can be made out for the industry in terms of employment". Since a SST is likely to be at the skill-intensive "end" of the aircraft industry, there is, in terms of employment creation, an even weaker case for Concorde than for other types of aircraft. The demand for skilled manpower from Concorde could be considered a cost rather than benefit.

'President Nixon's Review Committee on SST said in reference to the Research and Development programme for the Boeing 2707-300 "... this employment will be highly concentrated in professional, managerial, skilled, and semi-skilled occupations which in a period of full employment, when these skills are in short supply, may prove inflationary. Very few unskilled workers will be required" (p. H.10434).'

Technological spin-off fallacy

BAC's reaction to C. B. Edwards' 'cost-benefit, analysis' was reported in the *Daily Telegraph*, 22nd July, 1969:

> 'A spokesman for BAC said last night the Corporation had seen the report and considered it "fair assessment". But "it is an economist's view" and there are some things that cannot just be judged in book-keeping terms. We have never claimed we can recover all the research and development costs. But we don't regard that as a loss, only an investment in the technological development of the country.'

The statement is, however, characteristic of the effort to change the economic emphasis from one of straight profit to one of technological spin-off, fallout or by-product.

Mr Edwards pointed out:

'Few empirical studies have been made of the benefits arising from technological spin-off resulting from government research and development programmes. From those studies that have been carried out (see, e.g., refs. 15, 16 and 17) it is impossible even to estimate the benefits likely to arise from technological spin-off whether that knowledge is embodied in patents, registerable designs, copyrights, or just know-how (when the knowledge is not made the subject of property rights).

'The Plowden Report (Appendix J) gives examples of technological fallout, but in paragraph 172, it states that ". . . taking a long view, the technological fallout from the industry cannot be advanced as a major justification for support to ensure that the industry survives or is maintained at any particular level". A similar opinion was advanced by the Ministry of Technology officials interviewed. Although therefore, it is impossible to gauge the likely benefits which might result from cost-reducing or product-creating innovations developed as a result of Concorde, they are unlikely to be significant. In this respect, it seems worth again quoting the report of the USA's SST Review Committee, this time on the subject of technological spin-off or fallout. The report said that "The SST program will advance many areas of technology and will result in technological fallout both to the aircraft industry in general and to other industrial and military applications. The magnitude of this effect is very difficult to assess, but it appears to be small. Nevertheless, there are a number of areas which can be identified as having a high probability of potential benefit such as: flight control systems, structures, materials, aircraft engines, aerodynamics. While technological fallout will inevitably result from a complex, high technology program such as the SST development, *the value of this benefit appears to be limited. We believe technological fallout to be of relatively minor importance in this program and therefore should not be considered either wholly or in part as a basis for justifying the program.* In the SST program, fallout, or technological advance should be considered as a bonus or additional benefit from a program which must depend upon other reasons for its continuation." (Author's italics – see p. H.10436, ref. 80.)

'These remarks, it should be noted, refer to the development programme for an aircraft designed to fly at Mach. 3, whereas "the designers of the Concorde decided at a very early stage that to develop new materials needed for Mach. 2.5 and beyond, like steel and titanium, would be too big and too costly a step forward. They settled for Mach. 2.2 (since reduced to just over Mach. 2) to allow the use of well-developed aluminium alloys" (*Times* Supplement on Concorde – Tuesday, 4th March, 1969).

'There are therefore unlikely to be any significant benefits resulting from the development of new airframe materials. There may of course be some benefits spinning off from the £800m to £1,000m development programme – those could, for example, result from the use of titanium and special high-temperature resistant lubricating oils in the engine as well as the development of recent production techniques such as electro-chemical machining, and electro-beam welding – but it seems *reasonable to conclude that any benefits arising from the technological fallout from Concorde are likely to be very small relative to the total cost of the project*' (ref. 31).

The Balance of Payments effect

Mr Edwards continued:

'We are thus left with the Balance of Payments argument in favour of Concorde. This is that if the Concorde Project had not gone ahead, British airlines would sooner or later have been forced to purchase SSTs from abroad. This does not necessarily follow, but *if* this is valid, then sales of Concorde not only bring in foreign exchange through exports, but also through import substitution, and, the argument goes, since the UK still (despite devaluation in November 1967) has an overvalued currency these sales have a value to the economy greater than their market price would indicate. The argument is simple – the analysis could be complex.[3]

3. See the analysis set out in *Manual of Industrial Project Analysis in*

'In such an analysis, one should obviously consider not only the direct effects on the Balance of Payments, but also the indirect effects. However, because of the approximate nature of the cost estimates and other uncertainties surrounding the project, there seems little point in conducting a detailed analysis, especially as the relevant effect is unlikely to have a very big impact on any gain or loss from the aircraft.

'If, for example, the pound is assumed to be overvalued by, say, 10 per cent, we might want to attach a "shadow price" to foreign exchange of 1.1. This means that we are then saying that exports are more valuable *vis-à-vis* imports than the official rate of exchange would indicate, and that instead of the official rate of exchange of $2.8 to the £, we should use a "shadow" rate of something like $3.1 to the £. But what effect is this adjustment likely to make? If we assume a sales price per aircraft (plus spares) of something like £13m at the official rate of exchange, this represents a sales price of something like £14.3m at the "shadow" rate of exchange. The direct production cost per aircraft is likely to be something like £11m, giving a profit to the manufacturers of about £2m at the official rate of exchange. About 10–15 per cent of this cost is likely to consist of direct imports.[4] Therefore even if a "shadow price" of foreign exchange is used to reflect the advantage to the balance of payments, the "surplus" per aircraft is still only about £3m, and against this has to be set the vast research and

---

Developing Countries by Little and Mirrlees. Vol. II. O.E.C.D. 1969. Despite the manual's title, the methodology set out is appropriate for use in an analysis of the Concorde.

4. A publicity broadsheet produced by the British Aircraft Corporation (undated – it was being distributed in 1968) stated that 'about 10 per cent of the cost of a Concorde will be spent in the dollar area for raw materials and parts'.

'In February 1969 it was revealed that the French partners had awarded a contract for the Concorde's navigational equipment to a US company. This contract had been expected to go to Ferranti (of Edinburgh). At an estimated cost of £200,000 for each set of equipment, this *adds a further 3 per cent* of the cost of a Concorde to the amount to be spent in the dollar area'.

development costs which do themselves include imports.

'This calculation also assumes that the sales price will exceed the production cost, but there seems to be some doubt about this. In July 1969, Lord Beswick said in the House of Lords – "My Lords, the prospects for selling this aircraft are good, and if things go well, there is every prospect of recouping the economic cost of the *production* aircraft. But it has long been agreed . . . that it will not be possible to recover the cost of research and development." (Author's italics – *Hansard* – House of Lords, 16th July, 1969; col. 258.)

'In the same year, the SST Review Committee in the USA stated that "Cables from our embassies in London and Paris indicate that some French and British officials close to the programme are sceptical of the Concorde's commercial viability" (p. H.10433). And in November 1969, the Public Accounts Committee was reported as saying that "Your Committee were also informed that in consequence of the present cost escalation, the proportion of total development costs of Concorde which could now be recovered in the production price would probably be a good deal less than the one-third previously contemplated." (*Hansard*, 20th November, 1969; col. 1570.)

'Thus BAC's claim made in an *aide memoire* produced in 1969, that "a sale of 250 Concordes would bring into the UK and France some £2m each in foreign currency over the operating life of the aircraft (this figure includes in addition to the proceeds of export sales, the net overseas earnings of home-based Concordes)", seems at best mistaken, and at worst deliberately misleading. It excludes the adverse effects upon the UK and French balance of payments of the operation of *foreign*-owned Concordes (which BAC is presumably hoping it will sell), and the cost of each aircraft, a significant proportion of which will consist of imports.

'*Thus the balance of payments advantages of Concorde are likely to be insignificant*, and none of the 'non-quantifiable' benefits which are often invoked in support of Concorde is likely to amount to much, relative to the total research and development cost.'

CHAPTER TEN

The Prospects For Concorde

Concorde's makers and their supporters have claimed that its future will be decided by the results of the current supersonic flight testing programme: if the designers' calculations are correct to within one per cent, and the supersonic drag is as calculated, then the Concorde production models will be capable of transporting the full predicted payload across the Atlantic, with adequate reserves of fuel. Then, it has been assumed, world airlines will – and indeed will have to – buy Concordes. If the supersonic drag exceeds the calculated value, the Concorde will have failed; but the makers claim that they are confident the sums are correct – and that therefore Concorde must succeed.

But of course technical viability is only one of the factors which will decide the future of supersonic transport. During the late 1960s, 'environmetal' awareness increased enormously. In the same period, the advocates of SST have been forced increasingly on to the defensive. In December 1970, the opponents of SST have won some formidable – and possibly decisive – victories. On 3rd December, the US Senate voted to refuse further funding for the Boeing SST project. This was a dramatic reversal of the Senate's attitudes to previous appropriations for the SST. Senator William Proxmire, who, with Senators Edmund Muskie and Gaylord Nelson, led the 'environmentalist' opposition to the granting of the funds, 'said that the crucial element in the "turnaround" had been concern about the aircraft's impact on the environment – its noise on take-off, its boom at cruising speed, and the effect of its exhaust on the upper atmosphere' (*New York Times*, 4th December).

The *New York Times* commented in an editorial: 'The shift of a substantial number of Senators in both parties from their position a year ago is an encouraging testament to the power of an aroused public opinion. The vote demonstrates that if people care enough about defending the imperilled natural environment, their elected representatives will listen and take heed.'

The previous day (2nd December) in a somewhat frantic attempt to spike the guns of the environmentalists, the SST lobby, led by Senator Warren Magnuson, had themselves introduced a Bill to prohibit commercial supersonic flying over the US. An amendment was added to this Bill which limits the airport noise of SSTs to the level (108 EPNdB) set for subsonic aircraft. It is very unlikely that either the US SST or the Concorde can conform to this limit.

As the SST appropriation had already been approved by the House of Representatives, the Senate's decision has been referred to the joint Senate-House committee, and a compromise has been reached to cut the appropriation from the original $290m to $210m. This reduced amount will prevent immediate cancellation of the SST. But the message is clear: the Senate, and US public opinion, do not take seriously the claims about the benefits of supersonic transport – but they do take very seriously the environmental ill-effects it would bring.

On 4th December, Senators Muskey and Proxmire called for an international convention to consider the dangers to the environment that might result from the operation of fleets of SSTs.

On 6th December, Senator Nelson said that he intended to introduce legislation that would require future airliners to conform to strict noise and pollution standards.

On 1st December, 1970, under the headline 'US conservationist lobby poses threat to Concorde', *The Times* reported that 'The American opponents of the SST, encouraged by what they claim is their success in persuading the Federal Aviation Administration[1] to prohibit commercial supersonic flights over land, are now seeking to extend the ban to flights over the Atlantic. Such a move would directly affect the commerical prospects of the Concorde. Senator Gaylord Nelson . . . speaking at a news con-

1. This FAA regulation was formulated in April 1970.

ference . . . released a study of the impact of SSTs flying on Atlantic Ocean routes. The study was prepared by the Citizens' League against the Sonic Boom, the leading organization in the field, and other conservationist organizations. According to the League, a fleet of 50 SSTs in airline service would affect more than 60 per cent of the north Atlantic between Virginia and Labrador. This area would be hit by sonic booms as frequently as every 15 minutes. The study claims that the shock wave overpressure from the boom would be between two and four pounds a square foot . . . It notes that there have been no investigations of the effect of these repeated booms on marine and bird life, or persons on board ships.'

As Adam Raphael, Washington correspondent of *The Guardian*, wrote: 'Concorde's future may well then have to be determined by British and French Governments . . . on whether it has any chance of surviving "the new environmental politics". The prospects at this moment here seem dim' (The *Guardian*, 5th December).

Even before these recent moves in the Senate, the authorities controlling a number of US airports (including New York and Los Angeles) had stated that they would not allow any SSTs to operate at airports under their control.

The number of 'options' on Concorde, held by airlines, is 74.[2] Of these, 24 are with airlines whose operations are

2. Options on Concordes are held as follows:
Eight positions each for Air France, BOAC, Pan-Am.
Six positions each for American, Eastern, TWA, United.
Four positions each for Air Canada, Qantas.
Three positions each for Braniff, Continental, Japan, Lufthansa.
Two positions each for Air India, MEA, Sabena.

Total: 74. This number has remained unchanged for more than three years. The option-holding airlines have contributed less than 0.5 per cent of the estimated pre-production costs. In at least some cases, these small deposits have been written-off as advertising expenditure.

The number of options taken on the Boeing SST is 122. This has remained unchanged for three years.

In some instances the airlines have made advance payments of $1m 'risk money' per position. By September 1969 the total amount of such payments was $60m. This is only about 2 per cent of the total cost of the planes involved but provides a minimum factual basis for the FAA's claim that 'the airlines are participating in the financing'.

largely or entirely on the US domestic routes. Altogether, 36 of the options are held by US airlines. If it is impossible for Concorde to operate over, into or out of the USA, it is unlikely that many of these options can be confirmed.

About half of the world total of intercontinental air traffic is on routes to and from the USA. If SSTs are barred from these routes, their operability will be very drastically reduced even if no other countries impose such strict limits upon noise and pollution. But the attitudes which led to these limits in the US are rapidly developing in many other countries.

It is in this context that the airlines will have to decide, in the near future, whether or not to turn their options into orders. World airline profits are low; some are operating at a loss. Trans-World Airlines recently predicted at a meeting of its creditors that its losses in 1970 would be $60 to $65m (*Times* Business News, 17th December, 1970). The airlines are suffering the effects of having too many aircraft and too few passengers. Overcapacity on the north Atlantic is equivalent to 84 jumbo jets flying across, empty, each day.

Not surprisingly, several airline executives, including Mr Ross Stainton of BOAC, Mr F. C. Wiser of TWA, and Mr Najeeb Halaby of Pan American, have expressed serious doubts about the Concorde. On November 13th, 'Mr Knut Hammarskjold, director-general of the International Air Transport Association (IATA) today raised doubts about the short-term commercial prospects of the supersonic Concorde. Asked at a press conference whether he thought the airliner would ever fly commercially, Mr Hammarskjold said: "I do not know, but the international air transport industry has never before managed to absorb two new generations of aircraft in a single decade". This was a reference to the vast investments now being made into the Boeing 747 jumbo jet aircraft' (*The Times*, 14th November, 1970).

At Geneva, on 30th October, 1970, Mr F. C. Wiser, president of Trans-World Airlines, said 'that the Concorde would lose money unless the travelling public was willing to pay 30 to 40 per cent more than they now pay for first-class fares aross the Atlantic . . .' He emphasized that Concorde would be a 'a loser' because its sales price is too high and its payload too small . . . Mr Wiser said, however, that he could not rule out a TWA purchase of Concorde if both BOAC and Air France decided to put it into service (*New York Times*, 31st October, 1970).

Mr Wiser's last remark gives a clue to the tactics which the makers of the Concorde and their supporters were intending to use to start a landslide of Concorde orders. It was their intention (and probably still is their hope) that the British and French Governments should apply pressure to BOAC and Air France to persuade them to place orders; the assumption being that other airlines would be forced to follow suit. But Mr Wiser's speech preceded the disclosure of the full extent of TWA's operating losses, and the tactics for starting the sales landslide have been severely knocked sideways by the Senate decisions of early December. It remains to be seen how the airlines – including BOAC and Air France – will adapt to the new – and rapidly changing – situation.

The achievements of the environmentalists in the US Senate are immensely encouraging to their friends and allies throughout the world. These victories are likely to be followed by many more.

APPENDIX TWO

Reports By The Three Working Panels of the US President's SST *ad hoc* Review Committee

(*Note:* On 31st October, 1969, the long-withheld report of March 1969 by the President's SST *ad hoc* Review Committee was released to the public: it was reprinted in the 31st October *Congressional Record* (pp. H.10432–H.10446) at the request of Congressman S. R. Yates (D., Ill.). The main content is the set of four reports by the Committee's working panels, three of which are presented here in full. A summary prepared by the Department of Transportation staff is not included here, since a majority of the Committee members issued statements declaring that the summary was biased and misrepresented the views of the panels. Some of these critical statements are appended.)

Introductory remarks by Congressman S. R. Yates

Mr Yates: Mr Speaker, the Subcommittee on Appropriations, of which I am a member, recently completed its hearings on the Department of Transportation. Among the appropriations requests was one for the SST. It was at my request that there was included in the hearings the report of the SST *ad hoc* review committee which was stated to have been made available to President Nixon by the Department of Transportation before he announced his decision to continue with the SST programme. That report was made public today.

The report of that committee is so unfavourable to the

programme that I am amazed that President Nixon approved the request for the SST. The committee, which consisted of many of the ablest people in this administration, recommended overwhelmingly in favour of suspending work on the project.

The report rejects basic arguments used to justify the SST. It disputes that the balance of payments would be favourable; it casts doubt on the economic viability of the plane; it questions whether Americans will ever accept the jarring sonic bang which is an inseparable part of supersonic flight, it raises disturbing questions about the damaging effects the SST would have on the environment, it criticizes the two-headed conflicting role played by the FAA in acting as the guardian of the safety of the Nation's airways and of the aircraft using the airways. While acting at the same time as the principal supporter and loving promoter of an aircraft having such dubious value as the SST.

Mr Speaker, when President Kennedy launched the SST programme in 1963 he said: 'In no event will the Government investment be committed to exceed $750m.'

With the appropriation proposed for this year expenditures on the project will very nearly reach the limit set by President Kennedy, and if the appropriations scheduled to be made over the next five years are added, this aircraft will cost more than one-half billion dollars more than the amount that President Kennedy established. I believe this is the logical time to call a halt to the programme and I shall try to strike the appropriation in my committee.

Creation of the Committee and main witnesses

THE WHITE HOUSE,

Washington, 19th February, 1969.

Memorandum for Mr James Beggs.

I am establishing an *ad hoc* committee to review the Supersonic Transport programme in line with the recommendations given to me by Secretary Volpe.

I hereby appoint you the Chairman of this Committee.

The other members of the committee will be:

Mr Rocco Siciliano, Under Secretary of Commerce.

Dr Robert C. Seamans, Jr, Secretary of the Air Force.

Mr John Veneman, Under Secretary of HEW.

Mr Russell Train, Under Secretary of the Interior.

Mr Richard G. Kleindienst, Deputy Attorney General.

Mr Arnold Weber, Assistant Secretary of Labour.

Ambassador U. Alexis Johnson, Under Secretary of State.

Mr Paul Volcker, Under Secretary of the Treasury.

Dr Henry Houthakker, Member, Council of Economic Advisers.

Dr Lee A. DuBridge, National Science Adviser.

Mr Charles W. Harper, Deputy Associate Administrator of NASA.

The activities of this committee should be coordinated closely with the Bureau of the Budget.

RICHARD NIXON

WORKING PANEL COMPOSITION

(1) Balance of Payments and International Relations Panel Representatives from Treasury (Chairman), Commerce and State.

(2) Technological Fall-Out Panel – Representatives from the Office of Science and Technology (Chairman), Department of Defence, and NASA.

(3) Environmental and Sociological Impact Panel – Representatives from HEW (Chairman), Interior, and Office of Science and Technology.

(4) Economics Panel – Representatives from the Council of Economic Advisers (Chairman), Labour and Commerce.

WITNESSES WHO ADDRESSED THE COMMITTEE

Dr Arnold Moore, Director, Naval Warfare Analysis Group, Centre for Naval Analyses.

Mr Gerald Kraft, President, Charles River Associates.

Mr Najeeb Halaby, President, Pan American.

Mr Robert Rummel, Vice President, TWA.

Mr Harding Lawrence, President, Braniff.

Mr Karl Harr, Jr, President, Aerospace Industries Association.

Prof. William A. Shurcliff, Director, Citizens League Against the Sonic Boom.

Lt-Gen. Elwood R. Quesada, Chairman of the Board and President, L'Enfant Plaza Corps.

Report by panel on economics

The Economic Subcommittee is struck by the large amount of uncertainty connected with the SST programme. Almost every economic aspect of the programme reflects unverifiable matters of judgement with great variance in the opinion of experts. Probably the single most uncertain aspect of the whole programme relates to the uncertainty as to whether an SST can be built in the given time that will meet the specifications of being efficient, safe, and economical.

The record to date is not completely reassuring. After extensive study, the previous design was accepted as a good design that would produce an SST with the desired characteristics, but failed. While we are assured that the current design will succeed, the previous committee was given similar assurance. Assuming the prototype design meets its objectives, major innovations will still have to be made to produce an economical SST. Past commercial plane developments have never involved such a large jump in technology. In the case of commercial transports, a new type of metal – titanium – must be fabricated; a new type of guidance and electric control system must be developed; more efficient and quieter engines must be produced.

No doubt, all of the technical problems are eventually solvable, but how soon and at what cost? The record for new aircraft being designed to make technological jumps of this magnitude is confined strictly to military production. The record in those cases is not good. Production costs have often been more than three times what they were predicted to be. The record of civilian production of new planes has undoubtedly been much better. Most civilian jet transports have met their design goals with respect to performance and price and their performance has been improved during the economic life of the plane. However, these aircraft were designed from well known technology. For example, the 707 was a commercial adaptation of an already developed and well tested Air Force plane. The developmental experience with the Concorde gives little cause for optimism; developmental costs have more than doubled.

These comments do not mean that we believe that the plane cannot be built to meet the specifications at the forecasted costs but simply that there is a large element of doubt. If the forecasts turn out to be incorrect, costs could escalate considerably.

Demand

Estimating future demand involves another area of considerable uncertainty. Each element in the IDA model for forecasting demand involves large uncertainties and considerable elements of judgement in which reasonable people may come to considerably different opinions. Total demand for the SST will depend on total revenue passenger miles in the future. The IDA model basically forecasts the growth rate at approximately 10 per cent per year. Historical experience, especially the last few years, suggests that a higher rate would be more accurate. However, it should be noted that IDA forecast a higher rate in the near future and a lower rate in the more distant future.

Revenue passenger miles in 1968 were 30 per cent above IDA's forecast. If we extend IDA's rate of growth from that base level, total revenue passenger miles in 1969 will be 30 per cent higher than forecast with an increase of approximately 150 aircraft. However, airport congestion which has already reached serious proportions in international terminals such as Kennedy, may prevent this traffic growth from being achieved.

The market for supersonic transport will depend on the supersonic-subsonic split. This depends in turn on those markets which are open to supersonic flight, on the relative fare between supersonic and subsonic, and on how the public values time saved. The FAA has assumed that the public will pay one and a half times their hourly earnings to secure an hour's reduction in flight time. IDA, after having looked at some very sketchy evidence, concluded that the travellers value their time at their hourly earning rate. A 1967 PhD study done by Ruben Gronau at Columbia University under the direction of Gary Becker concluded on the basis of a very detailed statistical study of air travel time from New York City to other points that businessmen value their time in air travel at 0.4 times their average hourly family income and that pleasure travellers valued their time in aircraft travel at zero. On the other hand, earlier estimates by the airlines indicate value of time from 1.3 to 2.1 times earnings.

The effect of assuming different values of time is substantial. Under the base case for the FAA with consumers valuing their time at one and a half times their hourly earnings, 500 planes will be sold. If, on the other hand, IDA is correct and they value time at one times their hourly earnings, only 350 planes will be sold.

In summary, the great uncertainties relating to estimating the public's valuation of time leaves the projected market subject to wide error.

Whatever the value of time, the split between supersonic and subsonic would depend upon the relative fares. If supersonic fares equal subsonic, all or almost all will travel by supersonic. The FAA in their base case has assumed that supersonic will have a 25 per cent premium over the subsonic. The airlines are hoping for something less. The FAA predicted their relative fare position on the basis that the American SST seat costs would be roughly equal to the subsonic fares existing in 1965. They assumed that subsonic fares between 1965 and 1978 would decline in real terms by about 25 per cent, producing the 25 per cent differential. However, between 1965 and 1968 subsonic fares have already declined 18 per cent. If one assumes as did IDA and the FAA that fares decline by 1.8 per cent per year in the future, by 1978 the relative difference in supersonic and subsonic fares will grow to 36 per cent rather than 25 per cent. Such an increase in the difference between fares will reduce plane sales by about 150. However, airlines may be willing to accept a lower rate of return in order to preserve a 25 per cent fare differential, with the result that the same 500 planes will be sold.

These plane fares, however, are highly speculative. They, of course, depend on the price of the plane and its operating costs which as has been pointed out above are highly uncertain. Both IDA and the FAA feasibility study assumed that the Concorde would not compete in the same markets with SST. Since the Concorde will be introduced five years prior to the SST, it may secure a considerable market before the SST is introduced. While the SST is expected to have operating costs below those of the Concorde, it may not be able to secure lower fares.

International fares are set by unanimous agreement of IATA in which each airline has a vote. With many airlines having the Concorde and with two airlines being intimately connected with its production – BOAC and Air France – it seems unlikely that the SST will force supersonic fares below those that are economical for the Concorde and drive the Concorde out of the market – the FAA assumption. The Concorde will be sold for about half the price and will have half the seating capacity of an SST. Thus, two Concordes can be secured for each SST giving airlines an additional flexibility in scheduling. If fares are kept high enough to protect the Concorde so that both types of supersonic planes operate in the same markets at the same price, then they may split the market which will reduce SST sales from 500 to 250.

Another imponderable in the market forecast involves restrictions that might be imposed because of noise. The supersonic planes are by general agreement very noisy. Whether the planes will be permitted to land at major airports is uncertain. How much noise will the public tolerate? Problems clearly exist for Miami International, Boston's Logan Airport, and Los Angeles Airport. However, the planned or proposed construction of new airports may alleviate the problem. It is not clear how much of the added costs of new airports would be attributable to supersonic transports.

It should be noted that by the terms of the FAA-Boeing contract, Boeing establishes the price of the plane. Given the demand model specified, Boeing ... could make more money at a price of $40m than at a price of $37m. In fact, Boeing could maximize its profits if it charged about $48m. Such a price would reduce sales of planes to something under 350. This would in turn reduce government royalties to the point that the government barely got its money back.

Financing

Will the operation of the proposed US SST provide a sufficient rate of return to the airlines to insure purchase of 500 US SSTs?

Since the SST is more capital intensive than subsonic aircraft, it is more sensitive to lower earnings. The model assumes that the higher rate of return earned on long-haul operations in the past will continue during the SST period.

The predicted ROI for the airline depends on the airlines achieving a load factor of 58 per cent. This is relatively high compared to the experience of US international and territorial airlines during the last two years or even the average for the seven years.

If load factors were to continue at the 1968 level of 52.6 per cent throughout the SST period, 1978–90, the return of investment to the airlines would only be 22.2 per cent of the aircraft sales price compared to a ROI of 28.3 for the base case.

Statistics for the past seven years indicate that a lower overall load factor than 58 per cent should probably be used in evaluating the SST programme since this rate was achieved only once (1969) in the past seven years. The 1962–8 average of 55 per cent would yield an airline ROI of 25.2 per cent before taxes.

Financing the manufacture and purchases of the SST could prove more difficult than anticipated. It is generally accepted that the engine manufacturer will have the capacity to generate the necessary financing required. However, the EFR expresses some doubts regarding the airframe manufacturer: 'Pending receipt of the financial plan from the airframe manufacturer, a reasonable approach suggests that any programme decisions consider the possibility that the Government may be required to act as a guarantor of or to provide any additional funds needed by the airframe manufacturer.'

Requirements [In millions]	$
Facilities	278
Development costs	1,226
Leadtime production costs	1,295
Total	$3,429

Source of funds [In millions]	$
Government prototype participation	726
Airline prepayments	1,348
Tax considerations	310
Manufacturers shortage	1,045
Total	$3,429

'This situation is expected to continue through 1975 at which point a cumulative financing of $1,064m will exist . . . well in excess of twice the Boeing Company's net worth as of 31st December, 1965.'

Recent comments in the trade press indicate that the financing problem is more acute today due to increased costs and Boeing's additional developmental expenditures. The 747, 767, and SST programmes could strain Boeing's financial and managerial resources. If the SST programme is approved, Boeing might have to cut back some of its subsonic 767, 747, 727, or 707 activities.

The EFR assumed that the US airline industry could provide 86 per cent of its total cash requirements for the large subsonic and Concorde equipment cycle (1967–74) from internal cash generation (net income, depreciation, and disposal of flight equipment) and provide about 80 per cent of its requirements for the heavy SST start-up costs during 1975–7 from the same sources.

The recent decline in rates of return on investment (8.9 per cent in 1966, 7.7 per cent in 1967, and an estimated 6 per cent for 1968) suggests that the airline industry may already be overcapitalized. Declining earnings ratios will make it more difficult to obtain the large sums required for SSTs from internal sources and require more expensive commercial financing.

Employment

Under the FAA base case the SST programme may generate total employment, both direct and indirect, in excess of 100,000 workers, an unknown proportion of which will result from relative declines in other parts of the aerospace industry. This employment will be highly concentrated in professional, managerial, skilled, and semi-skilled occupations which in a period of full employment, when these skills are in short supply, may prove inflationary. Very few unskilled workers will be required. However, such employment should not be considered as a justification for proceeding with the programme but only as a dividend from it.

Report by panel on environmental and sociological impact

REPORT OF THE ENVIRONMENTAL AND SOCIOLOGICAL PANEL OF THE *ad hoc* SUPERSONIC TRANSPORT REVIEW COMMITTEE

Introduction

Supersonic transport (SST) has the potential for intensifying hazards to the passengers and crew for causing significant further deterioration in the environment for people on the ground particularly in the vicinity of SST airports and along SST flight paths. In recognition of their respective responsibilities in this regard in 1968, the Department of Health, Education, and Welfare established a 'Committee on Health Effects of Supersonic Transport', and the Department of the Interior assembled a 'Special Study Group on Noise and Sonic Boom in Relation to Man'. The Committee on Environmental Quality of the Federal Council for Science and Technology in July 1967 established a Task Force to report on noise as an environmental problem.

The Panel has drawn freely on the findings of each of these committees and has also been guided by the SST reports and briefings provided by the Department of Transportation.

The object of this report is to identify significant potential environmental and sociological problems related to the health and well-being of people which must be considered in making decisions concerning the SST. Technological, economic, and political factors both domestic and international traditionally considered in developing national policy with respect to such matters are insufficient with respect to the SST.

The Panel considers the principal environmental and sociological problem areas to be : (1) Sonic boom: (2) Airport noise; (3) Hazards to passengers and crew; and (4) Effects of water vapour in the stratosphere.

Sonic boom

All available information indicates that the effects of sonic boom are such as to be considered intolerable by a very high percentage of the people affected. The Panel is cognizant of statements and reports to the effect that supersonic flight over US continental land areas is not contemplated at this time and that SST design and development is proceeding on this assumption. However, the Panel is very concerned about the economic pressures that will be exerted if it is subsequently found that the economic success of the aircraft depends on over land flights at supersonic speeds. For this reason the Panel believes it is essential that the public be formally assured by appropriate authorities that commercial supersonic flights over land will not be permitted and that SST design, development, and economic considerations are and will remain restricted to over water routes.

Airport noise

The rapid growth of the air transportation system has resulted in a wave of public reaction to aircraft noise on and near major airports and many smaller ones around the world. The problem can be characterized as one of conflict between two groups – those who benefit from air transportation services and people who live and work in communities near airports. The conflict exists because social and economic costs resulting from aircraft noise are imposed upon certain land users in the vicinity of airports who receive no direct benefits.

'The development of methods to reduce engine noise is an essential element in the development of the SST as well as subsonic jet aircraft. Reduction of engine noise, however, is more difficult for the SST. Acceleration to supersonic speeds and efficient supersonic cruise require engines with high-temperature high-velocity jets. These engines are fundamentally noisier than the fan engines that are optimum for the subsonic jets.' (The SST Programme and Related National Benefits, 17th February, 1969, the Boeing Company, pages 6–22.)

According to estimates provided by the FAA, the levels of noise over a community on take-off directly under the flight path one mile beyond a 10,000 ft runway, with power reduced to hold a rate of climb of 500 ft per minute, are 111 PNdB (perceived noise in decibels) for the SST and 125 PNdB for the 707. On final approach one mile out from the runway the level for the SST is 109 PNdB and for the 707, 123 PNdB. For the SST the 100 PNdB contour extends laterally 6,000 ft on either side of the runway when the plane is 200 ft in the air at the end of the runway on take-off. The comparative 100 PNdB contour for the 707 is about 2,000 ft on either side of the runway. At the three mile point on take-off, the 100 PNdB contour extends about 2,000 ft on either side of the flight line for both the SST and the 707. By way of comparison, a trailer truck at highway speed has an overall sound level of about 90 dB at 20 ft, a pavement breaker about 115 dB at the operator's ear, and the values of 109 and 111 PNdB cited above for the SST are in the range of PNdB levels recorded indoors and outdoors during sonic bangs from B-58 aircraft. On the ground the SST is significantly noisier than the 707, the 100 PNdB contour extending about 5,000 ft in all directions at the starting point and from 5,000 to 6,000 ft on either side of the runway during take-off roll. The data indicate that on landing and take-off the SST can be expected to produce noise levels exceeding 100 PNdB over a distance of 13 miles. An area 4 miles long and approximately 2 miles wide surrounding the runway would be exposed to noise levels in excess of 100 PNdB.

Prolonged exposure to intense noise produces permanent hearing loss. Increasing numbers of competent investigators believe that such exposure may adversely affect other organic, sensory, and physiologic functions of the human body. Noise may also disrupt job performance by interfering with speech communication, distracting attention, and otherwise complicating the demands of the task. Such disruption could cause losses in overall efficiency or require increased effort and concentration to cope with the work situation. With regard to the latter, there appears to be a close relationship between bodily fatigue and noise exposure. Noise-induced hearing loss looms as a major health hazard in American industry. However, despite numerous efforts by professional standards and criteria committees, a national hearing conservation standard governing allowable or safe exposures remains to be established. Aside from hearing loss, noise may cause cardiovascular, glandular, respiratory, and neurologic changes, all of which are suggestive of a general stress reaction. Whether such reactions have pathologic consequences is not really known. However, there are growing indications, mainly in the foreign scientific literature, that routine exposures to intense industrial noise may lead to chronic physiological disturbances. Available information suggests that workers devoting constant attention to detail (e.g. quality inspection, console monitoring) may be most prone to distraction. Noise may mask auditory warning signals and thereby cause accidents or generate reactions of annoyance and general fatigue.

Although some reduction in SST engine noise may be expected to result from expanded research and development programmes on engine design and flight operating procedures, information available at this time indicates that land use planning in the vicinity of airports is the only satisfactory solution to this problem.

On the basis of the information summarized above, the panel is of the opinion that noise levels associated with SST operations will exceed 100 PNdB over large areas surrounding SST airports. It can be expected, therefore, that significant numbers of people will file complaints and resort to legal action, and that a very high percentage of the exposed population will find the noise intolerable and the apparent cause of a wide variety of adverse effects.

Hazards to passengers and crew

There is an urgent need to carefully evaluate the inherent operational and environmental hazards that will be encountered while accelerating from zero to Mach. 3 and cruising at supersonic speeds in a hostile environment. Passengers and crew will be vulnerable to a number of potentially serious physical, physiological, and psychological stresses associated with rapid acceleration, gravitational changes, reduced barometric pressure, increased ionizing radiation, temperature changes, and aircraft noise and vibration.

Man cannot tolerate acceleration loads above 4 to 5g. Visual disturbances occur between 3 and 4g. At 5g loss of consciousness occurs. Turbulent flight may cause brief linear acceleration of 10 to 12g which could cause fractures in unrestrained persons. Angular accelerations in turns and linear-angular accelerations during turbulent flight are important causes of motion sickness. Under cruise conditions the SSTs exterior skin temperature will approach 260°C, Therefore, it is necessary to insulate the cabin and to install refrigeration, whereas subsonic jets require heating at cruise altitudes because the external temperature is approximately 55 degrees below zero centigrade.

Ozone is present in a concentration of about 8 ppm at 65,000 ft. There is ample evidence that ozone is a highly toxic substance which must not be allowed to enter the plane.

A doubling of the present flight altitude reduces ambient air pressure from one-fifth to one-thirtieth that at sea-level. Therefore, in order to maintain current cabin pressures equivalent to an altitude of 7,500 ft, pressurization of the SST must be increased by approximately 2.5 lb/sq. in. above subsonic jets. A loss of pressure at 65,000 ft would result in all aboard losing consciousness within fifteen seconds.

The radiation hazard would be approximately 100 times greater than at ground level. A flight crew exposed for 600 hours annually will accumulate 0.85 rem (roentgen-equivalent-man) from this source alone. When this value is compared with the Maximum Permissible Dose of 0.5 rem for the general public the question arises whether SST crews should be placed in the category of radiation workers and kept under close surveillance. The advisability of allowing pregnant women especially in the first trimester, to travel in these planes, and of limiting diagnostic X-rays for individuals who fly SSTs will also need to be considered. Much higher rates of exposure associated with solar flares are to be avoided by utilizing a warning network which will permit the pilot to descend to safer altitudes. Criteria should be developed to guide prospective passengers afflicted with chronic diseases for whom the environmental stresses which might conceivably be encountered could be detrimental to their health. Lastly, special consideration should be given to the bio-instrumentation of flight crews in view of experiences in manned space flight which have demonstrated the occurrence of serious loss of insight and judgement which accompany stress such as hypoxia or fatigue. At the earliest indication of malfunction of the aircraft, especially in its pressurization, temperature control, or oxygen systems, the aircraft must be brought down to safe levels as quickly as possible either by the crew or by the automatic pilot. The health and welfare of crews and passengers are incomparably more dependent on the proper functioning of equipment for the SST than for subsonic aircraft.

Effects of water vapour in the stratosphere

The widespread use of supersonic transports will introduce large quantities of water vapour into the stratosphere. The weight of water vapour released is about 10 per cent greater than the weight of the fuel consumed. Four hundred SSTs flying four trips per day might release an amount of water vapour per day that is 0.025 per cent of that naturally present in the altitude range in which the flights occur. The introduction of this additional water vapour into the stratosphere can produce two effects which may be important:

(1) persistent contrails might form to such an extent that there would be a significant increase in cirrus clouds:

(2) There could be a significant increase in the relative humidity of the stratosphere even if there were no significant increase in the extent of cirrus cloudiness.

Both effects would alter the radiation balance and thereby possibly affect the general circulation of atmospheric components. Of greater significance may be the local contamination one can expect from a high concentration of flights over the North Atlantic. If half the activity is concentrated over 5 per cent of the earth's surface, local contamination would be ten times larger than calculated above on a global basis or about 0.25 per cent per day of the naturally present water vapour. However, the local concentration of water vapour from flights on crowded routes may spread out rapidly and be of no real significance.

Although it would appear that geophysical effects are probably minor, they certainly should not be neglected. Data required include information relevant to the horizontal mixing times within the stratosphere and to the resident time of gases within the stratosphere. With these parameters at hand, it should be possible to construct a numerical model of the stratosphere to determine more accurately the possible radiative effects on the general circulation.

The findings of the Committees referred to in the Introduction are contained in the following reports, copies of which have been provided to the *Ad Hoc* SST Review Committee Staff:

1. 'Noise – Sound Without Value,' Committee on Environmental Quality of the Federal Council for Science and Technology, September 1968.
2. 'Report to the Secretary of the Interior of the Special Study Group on Noise and Sonic Boom in Relation to Man.'
3. 'Supersonic Transport (SST) – Potential Health Hazards to the Crew, Passengers, and Population' (Unpublished Draft) Consumer Protection and Environmental Health Service, DHEW.

Report by panel on technological fallout

PURPOSE

To examine the importance of the SST programme to the overall national research and development posture, the technological fallout benefits that may result from the SST programme and specifically whether such benefits have security value.

SUMMARY CONCLUSION

The SST programme will advance many areas of technology and will result in technological fallout both to the aircraft industry in general and to other industrial and military applications. The magnitude of this effect is very difficult to assess, but it appears to be small. Nevertheless, there are a number of areas which can be identified as having a high probability of potential benefit, such as: flight control systems, structures, materials, aircraft engines, aerodynamics.

While technological fallout will inevitably result from a complex, high technology programme such as the SST development, the value of this benefit appears to be limited. We believe technological fallout to be of relatively minor importance in this programme and therefore should not be considered either wholly or in part as a basis for justifying the programme. In the SST programme, fallout or technological advancement should be considered as a bonus or additional benefit from a programme which must depend upon other reasons for its continuation.

These views are developed in greater detail in the sections which follow.

APPROACH

In order to develop a report responsive to the tasks outlined above, the following questions were considered:

1. What are the principal areas of technology which will be advanced by the SST prototype programme?
2. What value or importance do these technologies have to our national research and development posture?
3. What are the national security implications of technologies advanced by the SST programme? Are they unique to the SST or will other programmes provide similar benefits?

We shall discuss each in turn.

Question 1: What are the principal areas of technology which will be advanced by the SST prototype programme?

Aircraft technology will be advanced in a number of areas and this will enhance future development of both military and civil aircraft. There are aspects of this technology which will not only be beneficial to future aircraft development but should have more general application as well.

Aircraft Technology

1. *Aerodynamics* – The SST will require high aerodynamic efficiency over its complete speed range. Achievement of high levels of performance will provide useful correlation between theory and experiment, and extensive experience of use in the design of future aircraft.

2. *Advanced Flight Controls* – The SST demands on aircraft empty weight will assist in achieving advances in flight control systems which are being considered for other advanced subsonic aircraft. These advanced systems include: (*a*) fly-by-wire techniques which result in lower system weight than the conventional cable-pulley-hydraulic system. (*b*) Stability augmentation systems resulting in saving of aircraft weight through use of smaller control surfaces. (*c*) Control systems for suppression of flutter loading resulting in additional savings in aircraft structural weight.

3. *Aircraft Tyres* – In order to meet airline operational requirements, an improvement in aircraft tyres is required for the SST. The improvement expected will enhance tyre life in general and will be applicable broadly to other aircraft.

4. *High Temperature Structures* – The design of structures that operate at elevated temperatures is a relatively new field of engineering involving new materials, new manufacturing techniques, and new test methods. The knowledge and experience gained during the development and testing of the SST will contribute to this field.

5. *Aircraft Engines* – Realization of SST performance goals requires a significant advance in aircraft engine technology. Performance gains will result largely from operation at significantly higher internal cycle temperatures than have been used commercially in the past This area of improve-

ment must be accomplished without sacrificing engine life or maintenance characteristics normally associated with airline operations. Advanced noise suppression techniques are required if these advanced engines are to comply with evolving noise standards.

6. *Fuel Tank Sealants* – The high temperature environment of the SST fuel tanks necessitates the development of sealants usable to temperatures of 500°F. These compounds may find broader applicability in other aircraft applications.

7. *Environmental Control System* – The SST environmental control system will require advanced development of lightweight air compressors, small high-speed turbines, and lightweight, accurate, and reliable system controls.

General technology

1. *Metals and Alloys* – The SST Programme will create a new level of demand for titanium alloys which is expected to accelerate use of this very useful material over a broad spectrum of applications. High engine temperatures will require development of new high-temperature alloys.

2. *Metal Joining Techniques* – New techniques for metal joining are expected to be reduced to manufacturing practice in the SST Programme as a result of a need for efficient fabrication operations and in connexion with weight reduction. Diffusion bonding is a new metal joining technique which permits high strength joining of complex surfaces without parent metal strength reduction due to heating.

3. *High Temperature Nonmetallic Materials* – The severe high temperature environment of the SST necessitates development of new materials for use in this environment, including glass and lightweight composite structural materials made of plastic binders and boron or carbon fibres.

4. *High Temperature Seals* – The SST will represent the first use of hydrodynamic or hydrostatic seals in aircraft applications.

5. *Hydraulic Fluids and System Components and Lubricants* – Because of the temperatures encountered in the SST and the long life required, new types of fluids, lubricants, and system components must be developed which are

expected to have important industrial applications.

6. *Brakes* – the SST Programme is responsible for a search for new brake materials with improved heat-sink characteristics. These materials when developed would be broadly applicable to many different types of vehicles.

7. *Electrical System Components* – the high temperatures encountered by the SST require advanced development of wire insulation, antenna parts, and electrical system components capable of withstanding this severe environment.

Question 2: What value or importance do these technologies have to our national research and development posture?

It has been suggested that the technological benefits from the SST programme are impressive enough in themselves to provide strong justification for SST prototype development. It is our view that this statement unduly magnifies the significance and impact of the advances which will inevitably result from a high technology programme such as the SST. Although past experience has in many cases demonstrated that predictions of technological fallout can be extraordinarily conservative when projected over a number of years into the future, we nevertheless find claims for technological fallout from the SST Programme to be generally unconvincing. Many of the technologies are refinements of developments which had their origin in DoD or other aircraft programmes. Others appear to be of such a highly specialized character that broader application to other areas of the economy are limited, and in any event many years from being realized.

What then is the contribution of the SST Programme to our national research and development posture? It would appear to occur in two principal ways: manpower, challenge.

The Boeing Company has estimated that the design and prototype phase of the SST Programme will require a peak level employment of approximately 20,000 people, of which 3,400 are expected to be skilled engineers and technical personnel. This is about 7 per cent of the peak level employment in support of the Apollo programme. As in the case of Apollo, but to a lesser degree, the SST Programme, therefore, will both drain and stimulate the technical manpower pool in the US. We are not capable of judging the net positive or negative values in this area. For example, in the limited time available for this effort, it has not been possible to project other major programmes into the same time period to determine whether the manpower drain will be at the expense of programmes of potentially greater return. We have also not been able to judge the degree of stimulation to the training of future aeronautical engineers vital to the nation which may result from the existence of a visible and challenging SST development programme. We expect in any event that the most significant effect will, in fact, result from the second factor – challenge.

The SST Programme can provide considerable, but unmeasurable benefit because of the challenge, both in a technical and emotional sense, which such a competitive and forward-looking programme engenders. This sense of challenge, particularly if successfully met, can be a beneficial factor not only in the aircraft industry but also on a broader basis and on a national level.

In addition the technical challenge of a specific programme can serve as a useful focus for research and technology programmes and may thereby force new and important break-throughs.

Question 3: What are the national security implications of technologies advanced by the SST Programme? Are they unique to the SST or will other programmes provide similar benefits?

The question of whether the SST advances will have national security implications is relatively easy to answer. Of course defence capabilities will be enhanced by the technology advances made by the SST. What value can be placed on these benefits, however, is *much more* difficult to answer.

Both civil and military aircraft performance and efficiency are dependent upon the achievement of such factors as strong, lightweight structures, low aerodynamic drag and high thrust-to-weight engines with low fuel consumption. The SST Programme is directed towards achieving gains in these areas. To the extent the SST Programme is successful, there will undoubtedly be application of these results to help provide better military systems. In general, however, the technology rather than particular systems can be expected to be transferred to military use, because of different systems requirements.

In many areas, this technology interchange takes place from the military programme to the SST. For example, in titanium technology, the military have pioneered the use of this material for aircraft structures, such as the rear portion of the P-8 fighter, and the YF-12 and SR-71. The processing and manufacturing techniques being developed for the SST have their origin with these aircraft. Similarly, the two new fighter aircraft programmes being initiated, the F-14 and F-15, while of relatively lower performance than the SST and therefore not requiring titanium for its high temperature qualities, will nevertheless be one third to one half titanium by weight and will employ the latest design and fabrication techniques. These aircraft will have their first flights before the SST so this technology will be proceeding on a parallel basis.

Similarly, there are military programmes directed to developing better and lighter materials, for advanced engines, more efficient cooling and design features to increase aircraft engine temperatures, just as is being done in the SST. For example, DoD has a programme to develop new technology engines for the F-14 and F-15 that are more advanced technologically than the SST engine. These developments are essentially parallel to the SST engine programme, and are drawing from the same data base. Similarly the Advanced Manned Strategic Aircraft (AMSA) engine, even more advanced and coming in a later time period, will utilize the advances of both programmes.

Another development that has been indicated as mutually beneficial is the fly-by-wire control systems being developed for the SST. Similar systems are being developed for military aircraft. Both systems are directed at the same objective, the substitution of electrical connexions between the pilot and the controls for the present mechanical connexions. Weight savings, better reliability, and less susceptibility to enemy gun fire provide significant military advantages.

These are only a few of the many examples that can be cited of mutual interaction between the SST and military aircraft programmes, in which each programme benefits from the other. Specific applications are somewhat different in each area however, warranting separate approaches even though technology and principles are the same. Alternative approaches also provide the opportunity of developing new solutions to fundamental problems as a result of addressing these problems on multiple fronts.

In summary, the technologies advanced by the SST Programme will contribute to advancement in military weapons systems but military systems will not depend in a substantive way upon the SST for such improvements. The SST Programme cannot be considered as providing unique technological inputs to military programmes.

APPENDIX THREE

Part IV, The Supersonic Transport Development Programme, from the Report[1] of the Sub-Committee on Economy in Government of the Joint Economic Committee Congress of the United States (17th August, 1970)

Federal participation in the development of a commercial supersonic transport has aroused a great deal of controversy. Numerous attempts to analyse the public value of this programme have failed to produce a clear justification for Federal participation. Arguments have been advanced by responsible public officials that the development of a commercial SST would advance scientific knowledge, strengthen the US balance of payments, contribute to the health of our aerospace industry, provide employment and enhance our national prestige. Other equally responsible public officials have concluded that the SST would more likely hurt than help the balance of payments, would have a negligible impact on employment, would contribute seriously to noise pollution at airports, might potentially have serious effects on weather and climate, would be utilized by only a small fraction of our population, and is unlikely to be a commercial success. For example, the Under

1. Known as the Proxmire Committee, from its chairman, Senator William Proxmire, of the sub-committee's ten members, seven endorsed the report; there were two abstentions and one against.

Secretary of the Treasury for Monetary Affairs concluded in March 1969 that 'the balance of public benefits or losses may well be negative', and the Director of the Office of Science and Technology concluded that 'the Government should not be subsidizing a device which has neither commercial attractiveness nor public acceptance'.

In view of the many pressing demands on the Federal budget and in view of the recommendation of the Joint Economic Committee in its 1970 Annual Report that Congress take prompt action to meet 'the need to reduce or eliminate expenditures for space, the supersonic transport, and highways', the Subcommittee on Economy in Government in its May hearings undertook an extensive review of the social costs and benefits of the SST programme. We heard testimony from Federal officials responsible for the programme and from private experts. Representatives of the Boeing Co., which is building the SST prototype, declined our invitation to appear before the subcommittee, but made extensive written information available to us. The chairman of the subcommittee also requested and received written comments from the members of the *ad hoc* committee of Government officials which reviewed the SST programme at the President's request early in 1969. The subcommittee thus feels that its review of this programme has been quite thorough and that efforts have been made to obtain all points of view.

> *It is our conclusion that few significant public benefits appear likely to result from the supersonic transport development programme. On the other hand, very significant social costs are associated with this programme. More productive uses of Government resources are clearly available. No further Federal financial support of the supersonic transport development programme is justified at this time.*

The SST offers few public benefits

Employment Benefits of the SST. – The country is suffering from excessive and rising unemployment at the present time, and much of this unemployment is in the aerospace sector of the economy. We strongly advocate effective action to restore full employment. However, the employment impact of SST prototype development is extremely modest. The Boeing Co. estimates that the *production* phase of the SST programme will provide employment for 50,000 persons. This figure has been widely publicized, but it has seldom been pointed out in conjunction with this estimate that the production phase of the programme will not, at the earliest, be reached until the mid-1970s. The Under Secretary of Transportation stated during our hearings that 'the employment peaks in this programme would not occur until the latter half of the 1970s'.

The current phase of the programme, the *prototype* phase, is estimated by Boeing to employ 20,000 persons. This is only 0.02 per cent of the civilian labour force, and only 0.5 per cent of total employment in the electrical and transportation equipment industries. It is only 0.5 per cent of the 4 million unemployed in May 1970. The unemployment problems of this country can only be solved by promoting an economy which provides job opportunities on a much more massive scale, and this means productive jobs providing goods and services which society regards as useful and desirable. The SST does not qualify on these grounds.

Our conclusion with respect to the minimal employment impact of the SST is confirmed by the Assistant Secretary of Labour for Manpower, who wrote to the chairman of the subcommittee on 30th April, 1970, that 'although the overall employment situation in the country has certainly shifted since last year, we would still conclude that the net employment increase from the SST would be negligible'.

Balance of Payments. – The difficulty of estimating the balance-of-payments impact of the SST is evidenced by the widely different estimates made by competent and responsible Government officials. In testifying before us in May, the Under Secretary of Transportation estimated that SST sales could have a total favourable impact on the US trade balance through 1990 of as much as $16 billion. This estimate is based on assumed sales of at least 500 US SSTs and on the further assumption that in the absence of a US SST, the US airlines will import some 300 British–French Concordes. For reasons we discuss below, both of these sales assumptions are very hard to accept. Furthermore, this balance-of-payments estimate ignores the potential impact of the SST in generating increased foreign travel by US citizens. A more complete estimate of the balance-of-payments impact would consider the foreign travel impact as well as the direct impact of aircraft sales.

Using this broader method of estimation, both the Treasury and the State Department have concluded that the SST is at least as likely to hurt as to help the US balance of payments. In a letter to the chairman of this subcommittee on 1st May, 1970, the Under Secretary of the Treasury for Monetary Affairs confirmed his earlier judgement that 'the potentially adverse impact on our travel account from development of a US SST could equal or outweigh the positive impact on the aircraft sales account'. The Department of State also confirmed, in a letter to the chairman of the subcommittee on 7th May, 1970, that they continue to share this view that the balance-of-payments impact of the SST could well be adverse.

Competitive Threat Posed by the Concorde. – Many of the arguments advanced in support of the SST, especially those relating to the balance of payments, and the pre-eminence of the US aerospace industry, are based on the assumption that if a commercial US SST is not developed, a large and lucrative market will be lost to the British–French Concorde. Consequently, the subcommittee endeavoured to obtain as much information as possible concerning the Concorde. We found no convincing evidence that a commercially viable Concorde will be developed and sold on the world market in quantities sufficient to damage either our balance of payments or the health of our aerospace industry.

Although the Concorde prototype is now undergoing test flights, serious technical problems remain. It has not yet been demonstrated that the Concorde can carry passengers across the Atlantic without refuelling. The weight of the plane has increased substantially over original estimates, meaning that it must carry more fuel in order to give it trans-Atlantic range. It is quite possible that there will be no room left in the plane for any significant 'payload' (passenger and freight-carrying capacity). In such an event, substantial redesign of the plane would be required. It is not at all certain that the British and French Governments would continue with Concorde development in the face of another major cost increase.

Even if a commercial Concorde is developed and put on the market, purchase is not likely to be a commercially attractive proposition for the airlines. The British and French airlines, which are government-owned, can and probably will be required to buy the Concorde, and can be subsidized for operation of an uneconomic plane. In this event, other major airlines might feel obliged to purchase a few Concordes for competitive purposes even though they would be operated at a loss. However, the likely sales of the Concorde to US airlines are far below the 300 assumption on which some estimates of the impact on the US balance of payments have been based. World airlines currently have options for 74 Concordes, but these options represent a minimal financial investment and imply no obligation to actually buy these planes.

The Concorde does not pose a competitive threat of sufficient magnitude to justify continued Federal Government support of the US SST.

Scientific Advance. – The advance in scientific knowledge the so-called 'technological fallout', is undoubtedly useful, but this knowledge could be obtained in other ways, at lower cost. The Government officials who reviewed this question at the President's request last year concluded that 'the value of this benefit appears to be limited ... In the SST programme, fallout or technological advance should be considered as a bonus or additional benefit from a programme which must depend upon other reasons for its continuation.' This panel, which included a representative of the Department of Defence, further concluded that 'The SST programme cannot be considered as providing unique technological inputs to military programmes'. This conclusion was confirmed by the statement in a letter from the Department of Defence to the chairman of this subcommittee on 8th May, 1970, that 'there are other avenues of research which could develop the technology which would accrue from the SST'.

National Prestige. – As to the contribution of the SST to the health of the aerospace industry and the prestige of the United States, we find it hard to believe that either will be enhanced by spending billions of dollars to produce an aircraft which will have a seriously adverse environmental impact and for which the prospects of commercial success do not appear sufficiently bright to attract private financing. If our aerospace industry is to maintain its pre-eminent position it must do so by continuing to show the initiative to privately develop and finance products which can find a successful commercial market. When and if commercial supersonic flight becomes an attractive commercial proposition, private financing will be forthcoming. The appropriate Federal role is one of protection of the public interest by requiring that aircraft meet standards of safety and environmental quality. We can best enhance our national prestige and that of our aerospace industry by protecting the public interest.

The social costs of the SST are greater than is generally recognized

Actual Dollar Cost to the Federal Government. – The monetary cost to the Government of SST prototype development is now estimated to be about $1.3 billion, including the recently revealed cost growth of $76m. Some idea of the increase in cost of this programme since the initial decision to proceed with the programme can be obtained by comparing this $1.3 billion with the statement made by President Kennedy in 1963 that in no event would the cost to the Government be permitted to exceed $750m.

Numerous technical problems remain to be resolved

during the prototype phase – the basic structural material has recently been changed from titanium 'Stresskin' to aluminium brazed titanium honeycomb; a satisfactory fuel sealant has not yet been developed; and the engines still require substantial modifications to reduce take-off noise. With serious technical difficulties still to be overcome, experience with the development of other US aircraft, both military and commercial, and British–French experience with development of the Concorde all suggest that further substantial cost increases during the prototype phase must be expected. Cost estimates on the Concorde have now approximately quadrupled since the original estimate in 1962. Dr Richard Garwin, who recently headed a group of technical experts who reviewed the SST programme for the Office of Science and Technology, expressed the opinion during our hearings that a cost increase of 30 to 40 per cent over present estimates could be expected during the prototype phase of the US SST. Such an increase would bring the cost through the prototype phase to $1.7 or $1.8 billion.

Between $600 and $700m has been spent on the SST through the end of fiscal 1970. This is substantially less than one-half of what we regard as a realistic estimate of the costs through the prototype phase. Two hundred and ninety million dollars has been requested for fiscal year 1971. If the programme is terminated now, the cost to the Government, while large, would be only a fraction of the eventual total costs of prototype development.

Even more disturbing than the probable cost increase during the *prototype* phase is the likely need for Government support for the actual *production* of the aircraft. Financing requirements for the production phase were estimated by the Under Secretary of Transportation to be about twice those for the 747 jet, or about $1 billion. Although officials responsible for the programme have repeatedly expressed a belief that the production phase will be privately financed, they have been unable to produce evidence in support of this belief and unwilling to give a commitment that Federal support for SST production would not be sought. Indeed, the Under Secretary of Transportation expressed to us his intention to recommend Federal support of SST production, should that prove necessary, when he stated, 'I am on record ... with the statement that while I was of the opinion that private financing would be available, if it were not at that time, and if we felt that we had a successful SST programme. . .and it required some Government-guaranteed loans, then I would think that we would so recommend.'

Other witnesses expressed the belief that the total cost of SST development and production would be on the order of $5 to $7 billion. They expressed great scepticism about the availability of private financing, in the absence of Government guarantees. They felt that the Government's share of the cost of the SST programme might well reach $3 to $4 billion. This scepticism concerning private financing is due to the very shaky prospects of the SST for commercial success and to the readily available opportunities for private capital to find alternative uses which appear both safer and more profitable

Our witnesses felt that the estimates being used by the advocates of the programme that 500 or more SSTs can be sold were entirely unrealistic. The airlines have heavy financial commitments over the next several years for the purchase of 747s (jumbo jets). Operating costs for the 747 will be far below those for the SST. The number of travellers willing to pay the premium necessary to cover the higher cost of operation of the SST will be very small. In a tight financial situation and with more than adequate capacity already available, the airlines are unlikely to purchase many SSTs. For those SSTs which are put into commercial operation, fares are likely to be set below full cost of operation. This loss will probably be covered by keeping fares higher than otherwise necessary on subsonic flights. Thus, all air travellers will help subsidize the SST. Asked about the views of airline executives regarding the SST, Gen. Elwood Quesada, who is a director of American Airlines, told us, 'There are a lot of people that say that the airlines wish the [SST] aircraft would go away. And I am one of them.'

Adding to our scepticism about the commercial success of the SST and its ability to attract private financing is the apparent inability of the Boeing Co. to come up with a financial plan as required under its contract with the Government. The contract as amended in July 1969 required Boeing to submit by 31st December, 1969, a plan for financing of the production phase, but the subcommittee was informed that this requirement had been waived by mutual agreement until 30th June, 1972. Thus the Congress is being asked to appropriate $290m this year for a programme for which no assurance can be given that there is any upper limit on the eventual total cost to the Government.

The SST has sometimes been defended as an appropriate use of government money on the grounds that the Government will recover its investment. Even if it were correct that the Government investment will be fully recovered, this argument obviously does not justify Government participation in a programme. On the basis of this argument, the Government should feel free to invest in any commercial enterprise, just so long as the prospects for recovery of the investment were good. However, we have concluded that, in any case, the prospects of the Government fully recovering its investment are remote. The contract is designed to produce recovery of the Government dollars invested upon sale of the 300th SST. Subsequent royalties cease when the Government has earned 6 per cent on its investment. Thus, the maximum potential return to the Government under its contract with Boeing is recovery of its investment plus 6 per cent.[2] Six per cent is obviously not a full rate of return to capital in today's market. The average cost of Treasury borrowing has been consistently above 6 per cent since early 1969.

Should sales total less than 300 planes there is no assurance that the Government would get any money back at all. The contract already allows deferment of royalties, by

2. In a Summary of Current Economic Studies of the US Supersonic Transport prepared by the Federal Aviation Administration in September 1969, it was estimated that the Government's rate of return assuming the sale of 500 planes would be only 4.3 per cent, while the after tax rate of return for Boeing would be 15 per cent and for General Electric, the engine manufacturer, 11.2 per cent.

mutual agreement, until after 100 airframes have been sold. One can easily imagine further royalty deferment if poor sales are causing losses to the private investors. Another weakness of the contract is that it defines 'airframe' as one designed to fly at speeds between Mach. 2.2 and Mach. 3.1. Should Boeing redesign the aircraft to fly at Mach. 2.1, its financial obligation to the Government would apparently be terminated.

Our private witnesses did not feel the prospects for selling 300 SSTs were very bright. When we asked General Quesada how much the Government might lose if, for example, only 279 aircraft were sold, he replied, 'I think the Government in all probabilty would lose all of its investment.'

> *No satisfactory evidence has been presented that the production phase of the SST programme can be financed entirely from private sources. If the SST programme is continued, the total cost to the Government is likely to reach $3 billion or more. There is little prospect that the Government will earn a reasonable rate of return on its investment. It is entirely possible that the Government will recover none of this investment.*

Environmental Costs of the SST: Sonic Boom. – There are at least three major types of environmental cost associated with the SST. These are sonic boom, airport noise, and possible damaging effects on the upper atmosphere through the introduction of additional moisture and the destruction of ozone. In an effort to meet the sonic boom problem, the FAA has issued notice of a proposed rule prohibiting supersonic flight over populated areas. We regard strict adherence to such a rule as essential. This rule, however, will greatly reduce the prospects for commercial success of the SST since operation will be restricted to overseas routes. There is thus reason to expect that great pressure will be brought to bear to relax this rule, particularly if the SST does not prove commercially successful when restricted to overseas operation. The language of the proposed rule is such as to raise doubts that the rule would be adhered to in the face of such pressures. The notice of proposed rulemaking reads in part:

'Sonic boom producing flights over populated areas within the United States are believed to be economically and technologically "unnecessary" as that word is used in section 611 of the Federal Aviation Act of 1958. Traffic demand studies have concluded that from 500 to 800 supersonic transport aircraft will be in operation by the year 1990. Available studies conclude that these expected traffic demands are sufficient to ensure an economically viable supersonic transport, even assuming a sonic boom restriction of the kind proposed in this notice.

A restriction on sonic boom producing flights over populated areas is supported at this time by the inconclusive results of research concerning the effects of sonic boom on the surface environment.

Will this rule be adhered to if the belief that boom productive flights over populated areas are "economically unnecessary" does not prove to be correct?'

Airport Noise. – While the problem of airport noise created by the SST has not received nearly as much public attention as the sonic boom, the dimensions of this problem appear to us to be equally as serious. The high level of sideline noise on take-off may very well preclude use of many of our existing major airports for SST flights. The costs of airport modification and of construction of new airports designed to accommodate the SST will be enormous. These costs have not been taken into account in estimating the cost of the SST. Furthermore, new airports will have to be constructed at a considerable distance from major centres of population. The time spent travelling to the airport could largely negate the flight time savings achieved by flying at supersonic speeds.

The FAA has recently set a limit on sideline noise at take-off for new subsonic planes of 108 perceived noise decibels. In terms of the noise measures used by the FAA, the SST will be three to four times louder than this standard, and it will be four to five times louder than the 747. In terms of the noise measure cited by Dr Garwin in his testimony the SST will produce as much noise as the simultaneous take-off of 50 jumbo-jets satisfying the 108 perceived noise decibel requirement.

In testifying before us, Russell Train, Chairman of the Council on Environmental Quality, announced a commitment by the Administration that:

> 'The guidelines with respect to noise certification of the supersonic civilian transport should assure that the noise environment in the vicinity of airports at the time of the introduction of supersonics will not be degraded in any way.'

In the course of questioning, Mr Train revealed that in order to fulfil this commitment to avoid degradation of the noise environment, it will in all probability be necessary to prohibit the SST from landing at most of our existing major airports:

> 'I believe that if we set our standard for the supersonic aircraft in a way which ensured that the noise environment in and around our airports will not be degraded, that it will be exceedingly difficult if not impossible for the SST as presently designed and the Concorde as we now know it to operate from US airports.'

Eventually the technology necessary to overcome this noise problem will undoubtedly be developed. But such technology is not presently available, nor is an adequate effort to develop such technology apparently being undertaken. Mr Train told us:

> 'The present level of research in sideline noise, as well as the other environmental problems and uncertainties to which I have referred, is not at a level that we think it should be.'

Dr Gordon McDonald, a member of the Council on Environmental Quality, added:

'Using current technology, the chances of obtaining an economically viable airplane and meeting what we propose as the noise criterion are slim. However, there are alternatives ahead that might very well lead to a quieter engine.'

We strongly support the commitment made by the Administration that the supersonic transport will not be allowed to degrade the noise environment in the vicinity of airports. This commitment should be incorporated into regulations setting airport noise standards for supersonic planes; standards equally as stringent as those already established for new subsonic planes. The Congress should, however, be aware that unless new technology for reducing engine noise can be developed, adherence to this commitment will make it difficult or impossible for the SST to operate from existing US airports.

Atmospheric Effects. – The third major environmental problem associated with the SST, the possible damage to the upper atmosphere, has also received inadequate public attention. When the Chairman of the Council on Environmental Quality called this area of concern to the attention of our subcommittee, he made it clear that the possible effects on weather and climate are not well understood at this time. It is known that SST operation will introduce substantial additional moisture into the stratosphere. This moisture may destroy some fraction of the ozone in the atmosphere, leading to an increase in the ultraviolet radiation which reaches the earth. This moisture may also increase our cloud cover.

Mr Train told us:

'The increased water content coupled with the natural increase could lead in a few years to a sun shielding cloud cover with serious consequences on climate . . . The effects should be thoroughly understood before any country proceeds with a massive introduction of supersonic transports.'

With respect to the destruction of ozone and the consequent increase in ultraviolet radiation, little is known at this time about what the harmful effects might be. The ultraviolet radiation which presently reaches the earth causes such familiar effects as sunburn. Life could not exist on the surface of the earth if the earth were not shielded by ozone from the full effects of ultraviolet radiation. It is not presently known just what adverse effects small increases in ultraviolet radiation might have on leafy plants and sensitive life forms. Dr McDonald of the Council on Environmental Quality stated at our hearings:

> 'This is potentially such a significant problem that we really must understand it before proceeding in any way to alter the water vapour content of this part of the atmosphere.'

It seems clear to us that further work on the SST prototype is premature at this time. Research efforts should be concentrated on investigating the effects on weather and climate of introducing additional moisture into the stratosphere; on new technology to reduce engine noise; and on efforts to eliminate the sonic boom. When more progress has been made in overcoming these serious environmental effects, the SST may look like a much more attractive commercial proposition. When the SST does become an attractive commercial proposition, we believe that private financing will be available, and there will be no need for direct Government investment in SST development.

APPENDIX FOUR

OTHER COUNTRIES' ATTITUDES

USA

The Citizens' League against the Sonic Boom, and the Coalition against the SST (organized in the USA by Friends of the Earth) have been leading opposition to the development of the Boeing SST. The Coalition includes diverse groups representing conservationists, labour, consumers, etc.

On 8th January, 1970, the US President issued a policy statement against supersonic flights over land. On 16th April, 1970, the FAA published a 'Notice of Proposed Rule Making', 'Civil Aircraft Sonic Boom' (Docket 10261, Notice 70–16, publ. in Fed. Reg. Vol. 35, no 74). 'The Federal Aviation Administration is considering the amendment of Part 91 of the Federal Aviation Regulations to afford the public protection from civil aircraft sonic boom in accordance with the requirements of section 611 of the Federal Aviation Act of 1958 . . .

On 2nd December, 1970, the US Senate voted to prohibit commercial supersonic flights over the USA and to restrict SST noise levels at US airports.

EUROPE

At the first-ever international conference on the sonic bang, organized by the OECD at Paris in February 1970, five European nations indicated that they are unlikely to permit supersonic over-flying across their territories. These were Sweden, Norway, the Netherlands, West Germany, and Switzerland. The *Financial Times*, 4th February, 1970, reported:

'The Swedish delegation led the attack on supersonic flight, saying that research had shown that booms of more than one-tenth of a millibar, or 0.2 lb/sq. ft, in intensity must be judged intolerable to people living underneath.

In practice, this rules out any supersonic aircraft since the boom produced by the Concorde and the projected Boeing SST is unlikely to fall below one millibar, or 2 lb/sq. ft, in intensity and, according to some experts attending the conference, a reduction of more than 15 per cent in this level is technically impossible.

Indeed, the conference heard and accepted evidence which showed that certain unavoidable atmospheric conditions could magnify a sonic boom by up to four times its original intensity.

As might be expected, the British and French took a particularly defensive attitude throughout the meeting, arguing that the problem had been exaggerated and opposing the creation of any new mechanism for exchanging information on the subject.'

Sweden

Sweden was one of the first countries to institute regulations against sonic bangs that would damage property or awaken sleeping persons (per personal communication from P. Ahlmark, Member of the Swedish Parliament and initiator of the present regulations).

Mr H. Winberg, Director General of the Swedish Air Board, is very active. Mr B. Lundberg, 'father of all objections to the sonic bang', has represented the Swedish Government at many sonic bang conferences; his extensive series of analyses of sonic bang damage and annoyance are listed in the bibliography.

In 1967 the Swedish Government declared that 'civil supersonic flight over Sweden will be prohibited if the sonic bang causes regular sleep disturbance or damage to property' (ref. 61).

Switzerland

Switzerland has announced that sonic bangs intense enough to be annoying to people will not be permitted. The people have been warned that supersonic flights over their country could do many kinds of damage, including triggering avalanches (*Tribune de Geneve,* 20th December, 1967). Late in 1969 the opponents of sonic bangs were preparing to try to achieve an amendment (to the constitution) that would ban supersonic flight by commercial aircraft over Switzerland. (See Appendix 5.).

West Germany

'May I inform you that the German Government has stated on several occasions, that flight of civil aircraft at supersonic speed will not be tolerated if the intensity of the boom cannot be reduced significantly below the levels presently observed. Large scale annoyance of the public or damage to property will not be accepted' (letter of 2nd July, 1968, by the German Minister of Commerce).

Ireland

Preparations for limiting or banning sonic bangs from SSTs were announced in mid-September 1968 by the Honorable Erskine Childers, Minister for Transport and Power. He declared that sonic bangs could prove obnoxious and inimical to the tranquillity of the Irish countryside (*Irish Times*, mid-September 1968). He said: 'I am adamant that the tranquillity of this country should not be upset by sonic bangs and it is for this reason that I have decided to introduce legislation' (letter to W. A. Shurcliff of 15th October, 1968).

The proposed Irish legislation has been drafted, and is being held in readiness to be placed before Parliament if any threat of supersonic overflying should require its enactment.

France

French newspapers have given prominence to the 13 deaths of Frenchmen caused by sonic bangs. A 1967 report by French sonic bang experts mentions '... new and alarming evidence about the problem of the Concorde's sonic bang (Paris Bureau, *Baltimore News American*, 8th December, 1967).

In a poll, 35 per cent of the French citizens interrogated said they 'definitely could not' tolerate 10 bangs a day (ref. 14).

There is much general dissatisfaction with the large numbers of military sonic bangs to which the French have been exposed in plenty, but, as yet, there has been very little organized opposition.

In September 1970, M. Charles de Chambrun (Gaullist Deputy, and former Minister under General de Gaulle) presented a report to the Gaullist Party, seriously criticizing the Concorde and recommending that it be cancelled.

Canada

Canada has banned sonic bangs that would cause damage. On 10th November, 1967, Honourable Paul T. Hellyer, Canadian Minister of Transport, wrote to Mr E. Jervis Bloomfield of Ioco, British Columbia, that Section 515 of the Canadian Air Regulations provides that:

> 'No aircraft shall be flown in such a manner as to create a shockwave the effect of which is to create or is likely to create a hazard to other aircraft or to persons or property on the ground.'

Referring to questions as to whether the USA has permission to fly SSTs over Canada at supersonic speed, he wrote:

> '... I can assure you that no formal approach has been made to the Government of Canada for such permission and I can assure you that no such permission would be

given unless it were in the Canadian public interest to do so. In any case, all such flights would be subject to the Canadian Air Regulations including the section quoted above.'

Newspapers and individuals in Nova Scotia, Canada, have expressed alarm at the sonic bang threat since the shortest routes from many eastern US cities to Europe pass directly over Nova Scotia. See, for example, the main headline (in red!) of the Halifax *Chronicle-Herald* of 8th May, 1967.

Residents of Ottawa, Ontario, and Kelowna, British Columbia, have had first hand experience with sonic bang disasters in which $250,000 to $500,000 damage was done in a few seconds. (See Chapter 6.)

Bermuda

Bermuda may require SSTs – when at supersonic speed – to keep 100 miles away (letter of 6th May, 1969, from Chief Secretary of Bermuda to W. A. Shurcliff).

APPENDIX FIVE

ANTI-SONIC BANG GROUPS

The following organizations are opposed to the sonic bang of the SST or have at least given very serious consideration to the threat of the sonic bang.

American Speech and Hearing Association, 9030 Old Georgetown Road, Washington, DC, 20014. It sponsored the 14th June, 1968, National Conference on Noise as a Public Health Hazard, at which many speakers warned of the threat of the sonic bang. See *Proceedings* dated February 1969

Anti-Concorde Project, 70 Lytton Avenue, Letchworth, Herts, England. Richard Wiggs, Organizer. Issues newsletters and reports on sonic bang damage. Has published full-page advertisements in *The Times* and *Guardian*. Founded 1966, Issues pamphlets, reports, reprints, etc.

Association Nationale contre Les Bangs Supersoniques, 94 Boulevard Flandrin, Paris 16e, France.

Citizens League Against the Sonic Boom, 19 Appleton Street, Cambridge, Massachusetts, 02138. Dr William A. Shurcliff, Director. Dr J. T. Edsall, Deputy Director. Membership: 3,500. Founded 9th March, 1967. Issues fact-sheets, newsletters and 'SST and Sonic Bang Handbook'.

Comité Lyonnais contre le Bruit, Lyons, France. Prof. P. Mounier-Kuhn, President.

Conservation Foundation, 1250 Connecticut Avenue, NW, Washington, DC, 20036.

Cornwall. A. G. Harvey is organizing a group opposing SST overflights, at Penzance.

Eidgenössisches Aktionskomitee gegen den Uberschallknall ziviler Luftfahrzeuge, Schlossbergstrasse 22, Zollikon 8702, Switzerland. *President:* Dr Meinrad Schär. *Secretary:* Dr Andreas M. Rickenbach. Hopes to achieve, by popular vote, an amendment (to the constitution) which would ban supersonic flight by commercial aircraft over Switzerland.

Environmental Defence Fund, Inc, Post Office Building, Stony Brook, New York, New York, 11790.

Europaische Vereinigung gegen die schadlichen Auswirkungen des Luftverkehrs, Frankfurt.

Federation of Western Outdoor Clubs, 810 Hampshire Street, San Francisco, California, 94110.

Freeman, Mrs Arthur P., 3802 47 Street NE, Seattle, Washington, 98105. Organized an anti-airport-noise and anti-bang group in Washington.

Friends of the Earth, 451 Pacific Avenue, San Francisco, California, 94133. David Brower, President.

Friends of the Earth, 8 King Street, London WC2. Barclay Inglis, Director. Tel: (01) 836 0718.

Les Amis de la Terre, 25 Quai Voltaire, Paris 7, France. Alain Herve, President. Tel: 222–65–80.

Freunde der Erde, JM Bruggen 425, 8906 Bonstetten, Zurich, Switzerland. Eric Schindler. Tel: (051) 95–53–58.

International Congress for Noise Abatement (Association Internationale contre le Bruit), Zurich, Switzerland. At its fifth annual meeting (London, 18th May, 1968) it passed a resolution calling on all governments to ban supersonic flights by SSTs.

Lundberg, B., former Director General of the Aeronautical Research Institute of Sweden. Holbergsgatan 120, 161/57 Bromma, Sweden. Most competent and persevering critic of the SST and its sonic bang.

National Academy of Sciences, Committee on SST-Sonic Boom, 2101 Constitution Avenue, NW, Washington, DC. Dr John R. Dunning, Chairman of Committee. Reports and special releases have indicated that no avenue for large reduction in sonic bang is known and the present generation of SSTs will have considerably too intense a bang to be tolerated by people (ref. 8, 66, 67, 68, 69).

National Farmers Union branches in Pembrokeshire, Carmarthenshire and Cardiganshire have called for prohibition of supersonic over-flights.

National Organization to Insure a Sound-Controlled Environment (NOISE). Created in the fall of 1969 to oppose airport noise, sonic bang, etc.

Noise Abatement Society, 6 Old Bond Street, London W1. *Chairman*: John Connell.

Organization for Economic Cooperation and Development, Paris, France. Has published many reports on sonic bang damage and held several international conferences to consider the threat of the sonic bang.

Santa Barbara, California, City Council. First city to pass an ordinance against all sonic bangs. Ordinance 3246 approved 16th November, 1967 (ref. 39).

Schweizerische Liga gegen den Lärm, Sihlstrasse 17, 8001 Zurich, Switzerland.

Sierra Club, 1050 Mills Tower, San Francisco, California. Published several articles, and one formal resolution, against the SST's bang.

St David's Civic Society, St David's, Pembrokeshire – strongly opposed to supersonic flights overland. *Chairman*: Dr S. F. Logan Dahne, Garth, St David's.

UK Federation against Aircraft Nuisance. *Chairman:* Geoffrey Holmes, Chief Public Health Officer, Municipal Offices, Windsor, Berkshire.

Wilderness Society, 729 15th Street, NW, Washington, DC, 20005. At its 5th October, 1967, meeting it expressed concern over the SST's sonic bang. Its Resolution 12 urges that the production of sonic bangs over land by SSTs be banned (*Living Wilderness*, Autumn, 1967).

Bibliography

1 Acoustical Society of America, 'proceedings of the Sonic Boom Symposium', *Journal of the Acoustical Society of America*, No 39, May 1966, 80 pages.

2 *Aerospace Technology*, 20th May, 1968. Comprehensive account of the 1967 design of Boeing SST.

3 American Speech and Hearing Association, *Proceedings* of the 13–14 June, 1968, Washington, DC, National Conference on 'Noise as a Public Health Hazard'.

4 Anti-Concorde Project, miscellaneous newsletters, pamphlets, leaflets, etc., published by R. Wiggs, 70 Lytton Avenue, Letchworth, Herts, England.

5 *Aviation Week and Space Technology*, 28th October, 1968, 'Structure Critical for SST' and 'Eurocontrol Readies Procedures for SST'.

6 Baker, L., *The Guaranteed Society*, Macmillan, New York (1968), 276 pages.

7 Bauer, R. A., 'Some Thoughts on Human Response to Sonic Boom', talk given at 22nd October, 1968, meeting of American Institute of Aeronautics and Astronautics, in Philadelphia.

8 Baxter, W. F., 'The SST: From Watts to Harlem in Two Hours', *Stanford Law Review*, November 1968, pp. 1–57. Superb exposition of the physics of the sonic boom and the legal problems created by widespread damage to buildings and annoyance to people.

9 Bentley, B. M., 'The Sonic Boom', New England Research Centre, University of Connecticut, Storrs, Connecticut. A collection of excellent papers of several years ago.

9a Blackall, T. E., *Concorde – the story, the facts, the figures*, Foulis, 1969.

10 Bolt, Beranek, and Newman, Inc., 'Laboratory Tests of Subjective Reactions to Sonic Booms', by K. S. Pearsons and K. D. Kryter. Report NASA-CR-187, March 1965.

11 Booz, Allen, and Hamilton, Inc., 'Supersonic Transport Financial Planning Study', FAA Contract FA-SS-66-23; AD 652314; 16th May, 1967, 350 pages.

12 Boring, E. G., H. S. Langfeld and H. P. Weld, 'Foundations of Psychology', Wiley, 1948.
13 Borsky, P. N., National Opinion Research Centre Report 101, Part 2, 1965. AMRL-TR-65-37, Vol. II, AD-625332.
14 Brisson (Medecin-Lt-Col. de Brisson), 'Etude d'opinion sur le bang supersonique', Libr. Trans. 1159, Royal Aircraft Establishment. Says 35 per cent of French citizens interrogated said they 'definitely could not' tolerate ten bangs a day.
15 British Aircraft Corporation, 'Concorde', an 8-page newspaper-size brochure of 1968.
16 British Aircraft Corporation, 'Concorde supersonic flight testing and the sonic boom', 1969, 22 pages.

17 Carlson, H. W. and F. E. McLean, 'The Sonic Boom', *International Science & Technology*, 55, July 1966.
18 Caso, R. G., 'Town of Hempstead News', 8th October, 1968, and 9th October, 1968, statement presented to the FAA, pages 2 & 3.
19 Chacona, C. J., 'The High and the Mighty: the SST Charivari', Thesis, Harvard University, 1968, 35 pages.
20 Citizens League Against the Sonic Boom (CLASB), Fact-Sheet 10, March 1968.
21 CLASB, Fact-Sheet 11b, February 1968.
22 CLASB, Fact-Sheet 15, May 1968. Revised 1970.
23 CLASB, 'SST and Sonic Boom Handbook', 5th edition, 15th October, 1969, 80 pages.
24 'The Commercial Applications of US Aerospace Technology', Denver Research Institute, Colorado 1962–63 – Study carried out under a NASA contract.
26 Davis, John (Air Commodore), 'The Concorde Affair', 230 pages. Frewin (London), 1969.
27 Dickstein, Howard (Christ's College, Cambridge). 'Supersonic Transport and International Law', 4 pages. The Anti-Concorde Project, 1970.
28 Dwiggins, D., 'The SST: Here It Comes, Ready or Not', Doubleday, New York (1969), 294 pages.

29 'Economic Situation – a statement by HMG' – Prime Minister's Office, 26th October, 1964.
30 The 'Economist', London, 24th May, 1969, p. 70.

31 Edwards, C. B., 'Concorde, a Study in Cost-Benefit Analysis', Economics Department, University of East Anglia, 17 pages. Available through Anti-Concorde Project.

32 Fifth Report of the PAC – 1966–7 – paras. 40–53.

33 *Financial World* – 11th July, 1970.

34 General Electric Company brochure AEG-240R-6/68 (10M).

35 Gleason, G. K., 'The Supersonic Transport and the Boom Problem', Thesis for Harvard Law School Seminar on Legal Protection of Environmental Quality, 31st May, 1968, 166 pages.

36 Graves, C. Edward, 'Sonic Booms and Wilderness', *The Living Wilderness*, No 99, Winter 1967–8.

37 Harris, H. L., 'Assault on Emotional Health', *American Journal of Psychiatry 125*, 3rd September, 1968, page 159.

38 House of Commons, Official Report Parliamentary Debates (*Hansard*) Vol. 791, No 18, November 1969, HMSO.

39 Huard, L. A., 'The Roar, The Whine, The Boom and The Law: Some Legal Concerns about the SST', *Santa Clara Lawyer*, Spring 1969, 37 pages.

40 Institute for Defence Analyses, Inc., 'Economic Effects of the Sonic Boom', N. J. Asher, *et al.* , December 1964, AD 655608, 144 pages.

41 Institute for Defence Analyses, Inc., 'Demand Analysis for Air Travel by Supersonic Transport', Report R-118, December 1966, two volumes, AD-652309 and AD-652310. Indicates that perhaps 100 to 200 Boeing SSTs would be sold if overland supersonic flight were forbidden.

42 International Commission on Radiological Protection, Task Group on the Biological Effects of High-Energy Radiation, 'Radiobiological Aspects of the Supersonic Transport', *Health Physics 12*, 209–226 (1966). Detailed analysis of cosmic ray problem.

43 John A. Blume and Associates Research Division, 'Response of Structures to Sonic Booms Produced by XB-70, B-58 and F-104 Aircraft', J. A. Blume, *et al.*, Report 662003 of October 1967. Prepared for National Sonic Boom Evaluation Office.

44 Kryter, K. D. 'Sonic Booms from Supersonic Transport', *Science*, 24th January, 1969, page 359.

45 Landis, C., and W. A. Hunt, 'The Startle Reaction', Farrar and Rinehart, 1939.

46 Lardner, G. Jr, 'Supersonic Scandal', *New Republic*, 16th March, 1968.

47 Library of Congress, 'Policy Planning for Aeronautical Research and Development', Document 90, 89th Congress, 2nd Session, 19th May, 1966, 280 pages.

48 *Liverpool Journal of Commerce*, 11th December, 1967.

49 Lundberg, B., 'Speed and Safety in Civil Aviation', Aeronautical Research Institute of Sweden, Report FFA 94, Part I (Speed) and Part II (Safety), 1963.

50 Lundberg, B., 'Pros and Cons of Supersonic Aviation in Relation to Gains or Losses in the Combined Time-Comfort Consideration', *Journal of Royal Aeronautical Society 68*, September 1964.

51 Lundberg, B., 'Aviation Safety and the SST', *Astronautics & Aeronautics*, January 1965.

52 Lundberg, B., 'Supersonic Aviation, a Testcase for Democracy', *NATO's Fifteen Nations*, April–July 1965 issues.

53 Lundberg, B., 'The Menace of the Sonic Boom to Society and Civil Aviation', Aeronautical Research Institute of Sweden, Report FFA-PE-19, May 1966.

54 Lundberg, B., 'Atmospheric Magnification of Sonic Booms in the Oklahoma Tests', Aeronautical Research Institute of Sweden, Report 112 of June 1967.

55 Lundberg, B., 'The Uneconomic Unwanted SST', 15th August, 1967, 44 pages.

56 Lundberg, B., 'Observations Regarding the Acceptable Nominal Sonic Boom Overpressure in SST Operation Over Land', 30th August, 1968.

57 Lundberg, B., 'Observations Regarding the Sonic Boom in SST Operation Over Sea', BL Report 109-A of 16th September, 1968.

58 Lundberg, B., 'Acceptable Nominal Sonic Boom Overpressure in SST Operation Over Land and Sea', paper presented at 14th June, 1968, National Conference on Noise as a Public Health Hazard, American Speech & Hearing Association.

59 Lundberg, B., 'Implications and Justification of the SST', from 'The Sonic Boom', a 2nd October, 1968, symposium,

Nederlands Akoestisch Genootschap, Delft, Netherlands. Postbus 162, Publication No 15, April 1969, pages 33–69.
60 Lundberg, B., 'Summary Statement on the Unacceptability of the SST Sonic Boom Over Land and Sea and the Economic Losses of SST Operation Confined to Overseas Routes', BL Report 118, 24th October, 1969, 16 pages.
61 Lundberg, B., 'Is supersonic aviation compatible with the sound development of civil aviation?' Aer. Res. Inst. of Sweden, 1962. (Based on a paper with the same title given by the author at the Cranfield Soc. Symposium, September 1961.) 36 pages.

62 'Manual of Industrial Project Analysis in Developing Countries', Vol. II – OECD, 1969.
63 Management Today, August 1968.
64 Mohler, S. R., 'Ionizing Radiation and the SST', *Astronautics & Aeronautics,* September 1964.
65 Murphy, C. J. V., 'Boeing's Ordeal with the SST', *Fortune*, October 1968, page 129.

66 National Academy of Sciences, Committee on SST-Sonic Boom, 'Generation and Propagation of Sonic Boom', October 1967.
67 National Academy of Sciences, Committee on SST-Sonic Boom, 'Physical Effects of the Sonic Boom', February 1968.
68 National Academy of Sciences, Committee on SST-Sonic Boom, 'Human Responses to the Sonic Boom', June 1968.
69 National Academy of Sciences, Clarifying material called 'Statement of the Committee on SST-Sonic Boom', 19th August, 1968; prepared in response to CLASB request that a false conclusion in an earlier report be corrected.
70 National Sonic Boom Evaluation Office Report NSBEO-1-67, 'Sonic Boom Experiments at Edwards Air Force Base', Interim Report 28th July, 1967.
71 Newberry, C. S., 'Response of Buildings to Sonic Booms', *Journal of Sound and Vibration 6*, 406 (1967).
72 'The Nine Lives of Project Discord' – Insight article in *The Sunday Times*, 2nd March, 1969.
73 Noise Abatement Society, London. 'The Law on Noise', 1969, 71 pages.

74 Organization for Economic Cooperation and Development, Directorate for Scientific Affairs: 'The Sonic Boom and Its Implications for Public Policy', by the Secretariat, DAS/CSI/T/69.53, 53 pages, 20th June, 1969.
74a 'Report in Five Parts on the Sonic Boom', prepared in August 1969 by G. M. Lilley for OECD Conference on the Sonic Boom, 270 pages.

75 Pao, Y. H., and A. Goldburg, 'Clear Air Turbulence', Consultants Bureau, New York, New York, 1969.
76 Parent, M., 'Effets des vols supersoniques', 17-page article in *Les Monuments Historiques de la France*, XIV (1968), pages 5–21. Detailed account of sonic-boom damage to historic buildings. Illustrated.
English translation from the Anti-Concorde Project.
78 Parkhurst, F. S. Jr, 'Noise, Jets, and the Sonic Boom', 11th August, 1967, Guilford College, Greensboro, North Carolina. A thorough review with excellent bibliography.
79 'A pilot study on Technological Spillover from Defence Research and Development Activities' – a report prepared for the Ministry of Defence in August 1968.
80 President's SST *ad hoc* Review Committee, Report of March 1969 *Congressional Record*, 31st October, 1969, pp. H.10432–H.10446. A majority of the members, representing twelve agencies of the US Government, expressed opposition to the proposed Boeing SST programme.

81 'Report of the Committee of Inquiry into the Aircraft Industry' – under the Chairmanship of Lord Plowden 1964–5. Comnd. 2853 – HMSO.
82 Report by President Nixon's SST Review Committee. Printed in the Congressional Record, 31st October, 1969, pages H.10432 to H.10446.
83 Ruppenthal, K. M., 'The Supersonic Transport: Billion-Ballantine Books 1968. (Citizens League against the Sonic Boom – Mass., USA.)

84 'SST and Sonic Boom Handbook', William A. Shurcliff, Ballantine Books, 1968. (Citizens League against the Sonic Boom – Mass., USA.)
85 Stanford Research Institute 'Sonic Boom Experiments at Edwards Air Force Base', 28th July, 1967. Report ETU-6065. About 300 pages. Issued by National Sonic Boom

Evaluation Office, 1400 Wilson Boulevard, Arlington, Virginia.

86 Stanford Research Institute Report 'Preliminary Study of the Awakening and Startle Effects of Simulated Sonic Booms', J. S. Lukas and K. D. Kryter, April 1968, contract NSA-1-6193.

87 Sturmey, 'Cost curves and pricing in aircraft production', *Economic Journal*, 1964.

88 *Times* Supplement on Concorde – Tuesday, 4th March, 1969.

89 'Transfer of Aerospace Technology in the US – a critical review' – Arthur D. Little Inc., 1965 – prepared for the Committee of Inquiry into the Aircraft industry.

90 US Air Force booklet, 'Sonic Boom Background Information', 68–1, 1968. Explains that sonic booms from supersonic military planes can damage property and annoy people, and that an effort is made to minimize such flights.

91 US Army Human Engineering Laboratories, 'Criteria for Assessing Hearing Damage Risk from Impulse-Noise Exposure', Technical Memorandum 13–67 (AD.666206), August 1967. Comprehensive review of studies made here and abroad.

92 US Congress, *Hearings*, Department of Transportation Appropriations for 1968, 1024 pages.

93 US Congress, *Congressional Record*, 10th June, 1968, pp. H.4733–H.4790 (Monumental issue on sonic boom).

94 US Congress, *Hearings*, Department of Transportation and Related Agencies Appropriations for 1970, 354 pages.

95 US Congress, *Congressional Record*, 18th November, 1969, pp. H.10995–H.11032.

96 US Department of Agriculture Report, 'Effects of Simulated Sonic Booms on Reproduction and Behaviour of Farm-Raised Mink', ARS-44-200, June 1968.

97 US Department of Justice, letter of 1st April, 1968, by E. L. Weisl, Jr, on damage payments in Oklahoma City and elsewhere.

98 US Department of the Interior, Sonic Boom Study Group: 'Noise and Sonic Boom in Relation to Man', 4th November, 1968, 52 pages.

99 US Department of Transportation, FAA Report 'Final Programme Summary: Oklahoma City Sonic Boom Study',

Rpt. SST-65-3, 21st March, 1965. AD. 459601.

100 US Department of Transportation, Federal Aviation Administration, 'US Supersonic Transport: Economic Feasibility Report', April 1967, approximately 200 pages.

101 US Federal Aviation Agency 'United States Supersonic Transport Programme', Report SST-65-10, July 1965, 44 pages. A chronology.

102 US Federal Aviation Administration 'Tentative Airworthiness Standards for Supersonic Transports', Revised Ed., 1st January, 1969, 207 pages.

103 US National Aeronautics and Space Administration Report, 'Result of USAF–NASA–FAA Flight programme to Study Community Response to Sonic Booms in the Greater St Louis Area', C. W. Nixon and H. H. Hubbard, NASA TN-D-2705, May 1965.

104 US National Aeronautics and Space Administration Report 'Sonic Boom Measurements During Bomber Training Operations in the Chicago Area', D. A. Hilton, V. Huckel and D. J. Maglieri, NASA TN-D-3655, October 1966.

105 US National Aeronautics and Space Administration, NASA Sp-147, 12th April, 1967, 118 pages. A collection of highly technical papers on the sonic boom.

106 US National Aeronautics and Space Administration Report 'On Supersonic Vehicle Shapes for Reducing Auditory Response to Sonic Booms,' W. L. Howes, NASA-TMX-52294, 12th April, 1967.

107 US National Aeronautics and Space Administration 'Second Conference on Sonic Boom Research', NASA Sp-180. 9-10th May, 1968.

108 US Tenth Circuit Court of Appeals, decision of 8th March, 1969, in favour of Oklahoma City homeowners whose claims amounted to $93,705.93.

109 World Meteorological Organization, Technical Note No 89, 'Meteorological Problems in the Design and Operation of Supersonic Aircraft' (1967).

110 Welch (Dr Bruce Welch and Dr Annemarie S. Welch) 'Physiological effects of Noise' – 'presents, for the first time – all existing information on the disruption of our psychological and physiological equilibrium by all kinds of noise'. 1970. Plenum Press, New York, 345 pages.

111 Zimmerman, F. L., 'Supersonic Snow Job', Wall Street Journal, 9th February, 1967.

FRIENDS OF THE EARTH

Thomas L. Blair

The man-made environmental crisis which exists on this planet is only now being recognized as constituting the ultimate threat to Man's survival. Something needs to be done at once in order to avert the final catastrophe.

There are in Britain many individuals, researchers, and conservation organizations working hard to protect the Earth from man's abuse. These people are deserving of the support of a wider public committed to stand up for the environment, its heritage and its future, and to be counted as Friends of the Earth.

Action is required to replace the throw-away consumer philosophy with a way of life based on sound ecological principles. To place our faith in an economic system which ignores the need to come to terms with our environment is foolhardy.

Friends of the Earth Ltd, founded in London in 1970, believe that the conservationist's cause is good and his heart is in the right place, but that he deserves more effective power. We also believe that the ecological researchers cause is good, his head is in the right place, but that unless we act now on what he already knows, his work will have been in vain.

We are not just idealists, but we do have ideals. We place emphasis on practical action and we recognize the need for many new organizations to share the work. We are also aware of the need to give more help to existing conservation groups, which have been labouring long and hard. Our Earth is threatened and needs every friend it has.

FOE intends, firstly, to pursue an active publishing programme with Ballantine Books, to provide the best possible information, written for the intelligent layman, about the remedial action required to meet current threats to the environment. We intend to encourage further research aimed at a greater understanding of the impact on the Earth of Man and his technological society. We shall also urge action now, based on what is already known to resist the use of a given technology without proof that it will not cause lasting harm.

We believe that the proper application of science and humanity will enable us to shun projects to which mere technological achievement lends attraction.

Unhampered by any party-political allegiance, FOE will undertake substantial legislative activity, including lobbying and focusing public attention on critical issues. We will join other organizations in going to court to fight environmental abuse. We shall wage an all-out war on any interest which ignores the needs of the environment.

FOE's members will form specific task forces supported by teams of environmental experts and citizens' groups. The acronym FOE is appropriate: any friend of the earth must be the foe of whatever or whoever degrades the earth.

If these goals are yours, contact us by completing the form on the last page of this book and sending it to Friends of the Earth, 8 King Street, London WC2.

Friends of the Earth

UK
Friends of the Earth,
8 King Street,
London WC2
Tel: (01) 836 0718

France
Les Amis de la Terre,
25 Quai Voltaire,
Paris 7, France
Tel: 222 65 80

Switzerland
Freunde der Erde,
JM Bruggen 425,
8906 Bonstetten,
Zurich,
Switzerland
Tel: (051) 95 53 58

USA
Friends of the Earth,
30 East 42nd Street,
New York, NY, 10017
Tel: (212) 687 87 47

Friends of the Earth,
415 Pacific Avenue,
San Francisco, California 94133
Tel: (415) 391 4271

Friends of the Earth,
917 15th Street, NW,
Washington, DC, 20005
Tel: (202) 638 25 25

European Representative
Friends of the Earth,
52 Avenue des Champs-Elysees,
Paris 8, France
Tel: 010 331 359 0160

Friends of the Earth
8 King Street
London WC2

..I should like actively to participate in specific projects

..I should like to see FOE tackle such problems as

....

..I should like to be kept informed of other books by Friends of the Earth.

..I should like to contribute the sum of £............ to further your aims.

NAME ....

ADDRESS ....

....

....

OTHER BALLANTINE ENVIRONMENTAL TITLES

THE POPULATION BOMB *Professor Paul R. Ehrlich*

The book you can't afford not to read! Over-population is with us now and will be the root cause of major world problems unless it is brought under control. This book tells us what is likely to occur – and what can be done.

(6s) 30p

THE FRAIL OCEAN *Wesley Marx*

'A fascinating and important book. The obvious comparison is with Rachel Carson's *Silent Spring*, and I can only hope Mr Marx's book will be as widely read, and have a comparable impact.' – *New York Times*

(8s) 40p

MOMENT IN THE SUN *Robert and Leona Train Rienow*

A powerful, provocative book for those who care about what tomorrow might bring . . .

(8s) 40p

THE ENVIRONMENTAL HANDBOOK: An action guide for the UK

Edited by John Barr

The 1970s is our last chance for a future that makes ecological sense. This handbook focuses on some of the major problems of our deteriorating environment, explains the nature of ecology and – more important – suggests action that can be taken right now in any community, by any individual.

(8s) 40p